THE SATI JOURNAL

The Journal of the Sati Center for Buddhist Studies

Integrating Study and Practice

Volume

Sati Press 2011

The Sati Journal

The Sati Journal is a publication of the Sati Center for Buddhist Studies. This inaugural edition of the journal addresses the theme of integrating study and practice. We are committed to supporting the teachings and practices of the Buddha through meditation and study classes and printed materials. If you would like to support the publication of the journal or the Sati Center for Buddhist Studies, please consider visiting our website and making a donation or volunteering.

Editor in Chief: Gil Fronsdal
Managing Editor: Jeff Hardin
Design Editor: Diane Wilde of Wolfe Design Marketing
Editors: Carolyn Dille, Nona Olivia, Lori Wong, and Ven. Thanissaro Bhikkhu

The Sati Center for Buddhist Studies
108 Birch Street
Redwood City, CA 94062

Phone: 650-223-0311 (voicemail)
Website: www.sati.org
Email: satijournal@sati.org
        satipress@sati.org

As we are not able to mail out copies of the Journal, anyone who would like to receive a mailed copy can order it through Amazon or CreateSpace where it is available as a print-on-demand publication. The journal is also available for free in print at the Sati Center and as a PDF version on our website.

Contents

Editorial

GIL FRONSDAL

THE BUDDHA did not formulate his teaching for spectators. He offered teachings and practices that could be a path to the end of suffering, to Awakening. To walk this path one must understand the path. But to understand the path one must walk it. The study and the practice of Buddhism go hand in hand, mutually supporting each other.

The Sati Journal, as well as the Sati Center for Buddhist Studies, is dedicated to advancing our understanding of the Buddhist path through informed and reflective exploration of Buddhist teachings, practices, history, and scholarship. We aim to support the mutual integration of practice and study. We hope that this will add depth, breadth, and healthy challenge to our walking of the path.

For this inaugural issue we have asked some of the senior Western practitioners of *Theravāda* Buddhism to address the interplay between study and practice. One of the common themes of these writers is the value of understanding the early Buddhist teachings on their own terms, i.e., to try to put aside our own cultural perspectives and biases in favor of discovering what the Buddha meant. The better we understand what the Buddha actually taught, the better we can respectfully adopt, adapt, and challenge those teachings.

Studying Buddhism on its own terms can provide us with a significant reference point for understanding our selves. It can be quite difficult to see your own cultural conditioning. Not only can Buddhism help us to see this conditioning, it can help deconstruct it so we can experience that which is not conditioned. Ultimately we study Buddhism so we can go beyond Buddhism.

As we better understand both Buddhism and ourselves we can become more responsible in translating Buddhism for the modern world. In the West, at least, many of us are still part of the first wave of Western Buddhist practitioners. It would be good if we can create a reliable foundation for the waves of future practitioners.

May the articles of this first issue challenge you, be worthy of being challenged by you, and above all support you on the Path to freedom.

Learning from the Buddha

VEN. BHIKKHU BODHI

AT PRESENT, here in the United States, there has been a keen interest in Buddhism on many levels, but one of the factors that has persistently hindered the healthy growth of the *Dhamma* has been the sharp divide between scholars and practitioners. The gap that separates these two communities is sometimes so wide that it seems as if they inhabit different worlds. Many who consider themselves "Buddhist practitioners" identify Buddhist practice simply with the practice of meditation, pursued almost as an autonomous discipline separated from a broader commitment to the *Dhamma* as a path to spiritual emancipation. This sometimes leads to new interpretations of the teaching, which may mold the *Dhamma* into an ancient system of psychology, or a technology of alternative states of consciousness, or an "art of living," whose sole purpose is to live happily in the present life. Such approaches can certainly be beneficial as far as they go, but the problem is that they usually don't go far enough. Thus it often happens that the serious seeker soon detects, in such modern adaptations, a shortness of vision, a lack of depth, especially when these sanitized versions are set alongside the classical formulations of the teaching.

On the other hand, in our universities, academic scholars engage in advanced research into Buddhist texts, culture, and history, with mountains of texts and highways of electronic equipment at their fingertips. This approach can unearth a vast amount of precious information *about* Buddhism, but it frames Buddhism in purely objective terms as a cultural and historical phenomenon and thus leaves the researchers untouched by their research. No doubt, from the academic point of view such knowledge can be extremely important, and there are academic scholars who accept Buddhism as a personal system of faith and practice. But because this orientation, to be true to its premises, has to treat Buddhism as an objective field of study without concern for spiritual ends, the research it engenders need not have a personal impact on the investigator.

Thus, in America, the current fascination with Buddhism has tended to split into two factions. On one side there are practitioners who are earnest in their dedication to Buddhist practice but who often lack a clear understanding of Buddhist history, Buddhist texts, and Buddhist tenets, some even rejecting the study of texts as an entanglement in concepts and views. On the other side there are academic scholars who possess broad factual knowledge about Buddhism but lack faith in the *Dhamma* as a transformative path. In neither case do we find a concern to actually "learn from the Buddha."

The Union of Study and Practice

For the *Dhamma* to thrive on American soil, it is necessary to bring together faith, intellectual understanding, and practice into some kind of harmonious balance. To combine textual study and meditation practice within the encompassing framework of Buddhist faith is an approach that resonates with the Buddhist tradition itself. Several formulations in the texts underscore the importance of bringing these two wings of the Buddhist path into balance. One, found in such suttas as *Majjhima Nikāya* 95, states that one who acquires faith should approach a teacher to learn the *Dhamma*. Having heard the teaching, one retains it in mind. Then one examines the meaning to see how the teachings cohere with other teachings one has already learned, how they relate to one's own experience, and how they apply to one's life. Finally, when conviction becomes firm, one strives diligently to realize the truth revealed by the teaching until one directly sees the ultimate truth oneself. A simpler scheme, found in the Buddhist commentaries, arranges the main stages of the path into three categories: study (*pariyatti*), practice (*paṭipatti*), and realization (*paṭivedha*). One first studies the doctrine, then puts it into practice, and finally realizes the truth.

Both these formulations suggest that study of the *Dhamma* is the basis for practice and realization. How much study is necessary will differ from person to person, and also from one tradition to another. There are probably no hard and fixed rules invariably applicable to everyone. Some people can practice effectively and achieve success with minimal doctrinal knowledge. Others need a greater amount of knowledge. Still others are naturally inclined to study the *Dhamma* extensively and in depth. But for anybody, a clear understanding of the fundamentals is necessary for genuine progress. Comprehensive knowledge of the *Dhamma*, when supported by faith and connected with practice, has additional benefits. It both broadens one's understanding and enhances one's effectiveness as a teacher. It can also become an inspiring and elevating enterprise in its own right, opening one's eyes to the vastness and depth of the *Dhamma*.

Getting Clear about our Aim

Though we may learn from many teachers and Buddhist traditions, if the teachers under whom we study are properly qualified and the teachings they represent are authentic, we are ultimately learning from the Buddha himself; for in the final analysis all these teachings derive from the Buddha either directly or via the evolving stream of Buddhist tradition. As we set about learning the Buddha's teachings, it is good to take as one's guideline a statement of the great Chinese scholar-monk, Master Yinshun: "Our objective in learning the Buddha's teachings today should be the aim of the Buddha in spreading his teachings." The Buddha appeared in the world to lead us out of suffering and show us the way to the highest happiness and peace. People are naturally averse to suffering and desirous of happiness and peace. So why can't we achieve this on our own, by following the inclinations of our own minds? Why do we have to learn this from the Buddha? The reason is that our own minds are clouded over with ignorance and defilements. Our ideas are generally subject to the *vipallāsas*, the cognitive distortions, and are thus "topsy-turvy." Consequently, though we all wish to be happy, too often we live in a state of agitation and distress, creating a lot of suffering for ourselves and inflicting a lot of suffering on others. Even when we think of ourselves as happy, our happiness arises simply from our success in obtaining material security and the pleasures of the senses. Such happiness is thus extremely fragile and impermanent, a potential trigger of future suffering.

Through his deep wisdom, the Buddha understood that suffering and happiness originate from causes and conditions, and he also understood, clearly and thoroughly, precisely what causes and conditions lead respectively to suffering and happiness. Out of compassion, for forty-five years he taught these causes and conditions to the world, so that people could understand what is to be avoided and what is to be pursued. One of the constant frameworks of his teaching, clearly delineated in MN 114, is "what is to be cultivated" (*sevitabba*) and "what is not to be cultivated" (*asevitabba*). Thus in studying the Buddha's teachings, we should make a special point of learning how to distinguish those conditions that are harmful from those that are beneficial; we should understand what leads to suffering and what leads to happiness and peace. We should undertake this project with a twofold purpose in mind: first, to advance towards our own liberation from suffering, our own attainment of *nibbāna*; and second, to contribute effectively towards the welfare of others, to show others how to achieve their genuine welfare. This fulfills "the twofold good," one's own good and the good of others.

In learning the Buddha's teachings, we further have to understand how to apply them to our own life situations. Many of the teachings that we encounter in the early discourses were addressed to monks, people who had renounced the world to devote their time fully to the pursuit of the way. It would be a mistake for lay people to dismiss such teachings as irrelevant, for they do reveal the ultimate goal of the *Dhamma* and the practice leading to the goal. However, the Buddha did not intend them in all respects for lay people, and it would thus be a mistake for lay people to assume that to practice the *Dhamma* successfully *as lay people* they should emulate the practice of monks and nuns. This could breed internal conflict, feelings of guilt and unworthiness, and also generate tensions within the family and at the workplace.

I think there are reasonable grounds for the belief that during his teaching rounds the Buddha gave many more teachings to his lay disciples than are recorded in the texts we inherit. Since those who compiled and transmitted the *Dhamma* were monks (indeed, not even nuns), they naturally selected the discourses most relevant to their own concerns and probably let other discourses sink into oblivion. While such discourses may have been lost, and along with them useful teachings, we can discern the main principles of lay Buddhist practice in the discourses that have been preserved. Of particular importance for lay practitioners are the Sigalovāda Sutta (*Dīgha Nikāya* 31) and, especially, many short suttas in the *Aṅguttara Nikāya*.

In looking to these teachings for guidance, we need to steer a middle course between two extremes. One is literalism and rigid conservatism, a strict and unthinking insistence upon the old formulations without making an intelligent attempt to understand their purpose and the conditions under which they were given. The other is unconstrained revisionism, which freely bends the teachings to adapt them to present circumstances. A healthy approach to the *Dhamma* would recognize that, while the doctrine itself must be applied in accordance with the time, place, and person, the formulations express timeless principles and thus should not be tinkered with. The interpretation and application must keep pace with the inevitable changes in human thought, culture, and historical conditions, yet they must remain faithful to the pillars of the *Dhamma*, to the extent that we can extract them from the texts.

Two Aspects of Dhamma Practice

The practice of the *Dhamma* involves two complementary processes that should ideally run parallel. I call these *self-transformation* and *self-transcendence*. To learn from the Buddha in a practical way primarily means to learn how to implement these two processes.

The final goal of the Dharma, enlightenment or liberation, is attained through an act of self-transcendence, an act by which we step beyond the limits and boundaries of the conditioned mind and penetrate the unconditioned truth. This act is exercised by wisdom. However, liberating wisdom can arise only when our behavior is regulated by ethical guidelines and our minds nurtured through meditative cultivation. To regulate our behavior and nurture our minds is the work of self-transformation.

Self-transformation means the methodical effort to cultivate ourselves in order to promote the arising of genuine wisdom. Self-transformation in turn is a double process. One aspect consists in elimination, the other in development.

"Elimination" (*pahāna*) comes about by the control and removal of unwholesome qualities. It means that we avoid unwholesome actions of body, speech, and mind; that we subdue unwholesome thoughts; that we repudiate false views. The unwholesome mental qualities, which are the springs of unwholesome behavior, are technically called *kilesas*, defilements or afflictions. Just as a gardener who wants to cultivate a beautiful flower garden must first eliminate the weeds and rubbish, so we have to remove the weeds and rubbish—the defilements—from our minds. The Buddha's teachings hold up a mirror to our minds and hearts, revealing to us the defilements that bring harm to ourselves and to others. By studying these teachings, we gain a better understanding of our weaknesses, the defects we must strive to overcome.

When we study the *Dhamma*, we also learn the methods to overcome them. This is one of the extraordinary strengths of the Buddha's teachings. They offer us a remarkable variety of potent medicines to eliminate the illnesses of our minds. What is so astounding in the early Buddhist teachings is their incredibly detailed insight into the mind. However, the teachings explore the mind from a different angle than we encounter in Western psychology. Their aim is not so much to restore pathologically disturbed psyches to functional normality as it is to enable conventionally normal people to rise above their limitations and achieve the utterly purified and awakened mind.

The Buddha's teaching offers us not only an analysis of our defects, but a catalogue of our hidden strengths and of the means to make these potential strengths real and effective. The Buddha has bestowed on us an extraordinarily pragmatic teaching that we can apply to our everyday lives and thereby gradually advance towards ultimate realization.

To move in this direction brings us to the second aspect of self-transformation, which is development (*bhāvanā*). The *Pāli* word *bhāvanā* means the cultivation of wholesome qualities, which promote inner happiness and make us effective channels for bringing peace and happiness to others. The *Dhamma* offers a wide range of wholesome practices, ranging from generosity and simple moral precepts to such schemes as the five spiritual faculties, the eight path factors, and the six or ten *pāramitās*. To learn these, we need to study the texts extensively and in depth, always inquiring how we can apply such practices to our lives in the most realistic and beneficial manner.

The second major process that we learn from the Buddha is what I have called *self-transcendence*. Though the Buddha speaks about eliminating unwholesome qualities and developing wholesome qualities, his teaching does not aim merely at making us happy and contented people within the limits of mundane life. He points us towards a world-transcendent goal: the unconditioned dimension, *nibbāna*, the calm and quiescent state beyond birth, old age, suffering, and death. This goal can be achieved only by a clear understanding of the real nature of things, the true characteristics of phenomena. The real nature of things has to be penetrated by direct experience, but we need specific guidelines to gain penetrative insight. While the goal itself may transcend concepts and ideas, the Buddha and the great Buddhist masters have provided us with a wide variety of "photographs" that enable us to gain glimpses into the real nature of things. None of these "pictures" can capture it completely, but they do convey an idea of the things we should be looking for, the principles we need to understand, and the goal towards which we should be working.

To engage in a study of the principles relevant to self-transcendence is a philosophical enterprise, but this is not philosophy as mere idle speculation. For Buddhism, philosophy is an attempt to fathom the real nature of things, to use concepts and ideas to obtain a direct vision of the truth that transcends all concepts and ideas. Buddhist philosophy is a great stream flowing from the Buddha, continually revised, broadened, and refined to bring to light different facets of reality, to expose to the light of wisdom different aspects of a truth that can never be adequately captured by any system.

When we study Buddhist philosophy, we must always remember that these philosophical investigations are not intended merely to satisfy intellectual curiosity. Their purpose is to aid in the task of self-transcendence. They do this by pinpointing the nature of the wisdom we need to obliterate ignorance, the primary root of all bondage and suffering. Ultimately they lead us to see that all the factors of our being, everything we identify with or become attached to, do not exist in the way they appear. Contrary to our untutored assumptions, which take them to be "mine, I, and my self," insight reveals them to be "not mine, not I, not my self." And this insight culminates in the abandoning of all acts of identification, all appropriation deriving from the standpoint of the subjective ego.

Learning the Buddha's Mind

I have been speaking about "learning from the Buddha" as if this always involves the study of teachings explicitly recorded in texts. But that is only part of what it means to learn from the Buddha. To learn from the Buddha means not only to study his words. It also means to learn from his conduct and his mind. Buddhist tradition has left us many records of the Buddha's deeds, both in his final lifetime as a great teacher and in his past lives as a *bodhisattva*, a seeker of enlightenment. These reveal to us the life, deeds, aspirations, and achievements of the being we call the Buddha.

The life, conduct, and mind of the Buddha establish for us an ideal standard that we, as his followers, should try to embody in our own lives. The Buddha stands before us as a human being who had been an ordinary person like ourselves, but who, by strenuous effort, had reached the pinnacle of human perfection. To learn from the Buddha we should not only try to find out what the Buddha taught in words. We should also try to mold our own lives in accordance with his qualities: his immaculate purity, his unhindered spiritual freedom, his great wisdom, and his boundless compassion. To learn from the Buddha ultimately means that we learn to be *buddha*, awakened human beings, pure, wise, and compassionate, peaceful and magnanimous. To advance in that direction should be our purpose in studying and practicing the *Dhamma*.

Ven. Bhikkhu Bodhi is an American Buddhist monk originally from New York City. After serving as a monk in Sri Lanka for twenty-four years, he now lives at Chuang Yen Monastery in upstate New York. Ven. Bodhi is a prolific writer of Buddhist essays and books and has translated and commented extensively on the *Pāli* suttas. He has just finished a complete translation of the *Aṅguttara Nikāya* which will be published by Wisdom Publications.

Learning from the Therīgāthā: What Liberated the Venerable Nun Uttamā

NONA (SARANA) OLIVIA

THE *THERĪGĀTHĀ* has seen increased popularity over the past years. Susan Murcott's 1991 book, *The First Buddhist Women: Poems and Stories of Awakening,* has made the verses of the elder nuns readily available to the popular market, coinciding with the burgeoning interest in women's role in Buddhism. With the recent controversy surrounding the ordination of women, many turn to the verses from these ancient female monastics (*bhikkhunīs*) as proof of their early existence.

As historians of women's writing have long pointed out, sometimes readers become so focused on the fact that an author of an ancient text is female that they lose sight of the content of the text. Understandably, contemporary readers of the *Therīgāthā* approach these poems as examples of a long lost female voice. No doubt, the dearth of ancient texts authored by women can give the impression that women did not compose, but the fact that the *Therīgāthā* was first and long an oral text is evidence of the contrary. As Rita Gross points out in her pivotal work, *Buddhism After Patriarchy*:

> Early Indian Buddhism also preserved, despite mainly androcentric record keeping practices, a remarkable document which may record more from women, from an earlier period, than any other set of religious literature. This document is, of course, the *Therīgāthā* .... Here is a clear, unambiguous, and straightforward

account, from women with high spiritual achievements, of what Buddhism meant to them, of the freedom and joy they eventually found in its practice (51).

We are indeed fortunate that any texts composed by ancient women have been preserved. However, we should not let our gratitude for these female voices lead us into projecting our values anachronistically and observing only their "femaleness." In order to understand the lives of these women who lived in ancient India, it is necessary to read the *Therīgāthā* within its specific cultural and historical contexts. Not doing so does an injustice to the poems of these female disciples.

There is also a trend to approach the verses of the *Therīgāthā* as evidence of what some refer to as "the feminine," a quasi-Jungian term popularized in early second-wave feminism. However, as many women of color and those of non-European ancestry pointed out then, the notion of an essential "feminine" naively assumes cultural, racial, and class norms that exclude the voices of those who do not possess these culturally specific idealized qualities. There is no universal "feminine." While one's sexual organs are anatomical, much of what we consider as gender norms are actually social constructions inscribed by an individual's culture. To borrow from the Mahayana *Vimalakīrtinirdeśa Sūtra*, Śāriputra asks a Goddess "Why don't you change your female sex?" The Goddess replies:

> I have been here twelve years
> and have looked for the innate
> characteristics of the female sex and haven't
> been able to find them.
> (quoted in *Buddhism After Patriarchy*)

I suggest that we not read the *Therīgāthā* as primarily historical accounts of these 6th century BCE women's lives; it is not their femaleness that these ancient women want to emphasize in their poems. The point of their Buddhist practice was not to reify any condition but to be free from clinging. Without clinging, a person can become more independent from what is culturally considered normative or ideal. By recognizing a deeper truth, each person can be him or herself without needing to conform to encultured gender norms. Most importantly, these verses emphasize the Buddha's teaching in the *Pāli* canon, and in remarkably powerful ways—ways that make clear these women received, practiced, were liberated by, and taught the same teachings we receive today.

These nuns lived contemporaneous to the historic Buddha. In some of the verses, they describe their pre-monastic lives as wives, mothers, daughters, concubines, and prostitutes. These snapshots allow us a brief look into the background—and the suffering—which drew these women to the *Dhamma*. Regardless of our gender, we can relate to these women, as when Vasitthi writes about her grief at the death of her son, "Grief stricken for my son, totally mad, out of my senses..." (133). We recognize the conceit of youth in this line from Vimala, "Young, intoxicated by my lovely skin, my figure, my beauty and fame, I despised other women" (72). By contrast, on aging, AmbāPāli writes: "Formally my body looked beautiful, like a well-polished sheet of gold; now it is covered with very fine wrinkles" (266). And of course many practitioners sympathize with the unnamed *bhikkhunī* who wrote, "It is 25 years since I went forth. Not even for the duration of a snap of the fingers have I obtained stilling of the mind" (67). These lines are only part of their stories, however, because each goes on to tell of the practices that lead to her release from suffering.

There are 73 verses collected in the *Therīgāthā*, each one from or about a different nun. In this brief essay, we will focus on one of these early nuns who gives us a glimpse into which of the Buddha's teachings the nuns' taught to each other.

Uttamā

According to Carolyn Rhys David's translation of the commentarial biographies, the nun Uttamā's father was the Treasurer of Savatthi, so we can assume she came from an affluent family. During her teenage years, she heard teachings given by the nun, Patacara that inspired Uttamā to ordain in the Buddha's *Sangha*. She was unable to make progress in her meditations, however, so she approached Patacara for help. In the following verse, Uttamā describes the teachings she received from Patacara, and tells us that she practiced these teachings and became free.

Uttamā's Verse

> Four of five times I went out of my room, not having obtained peace of mind.
> I had no control over my mind.
> I went to a nun who I trusted. She taught me the *Dhamma*, the aggregates, the six senses, and the elements (*khandhāyatanadhātuyo*).
> I listened to her teachings and then sat cross-legged for seven days, consigned to joy and happiness. On the eighth day I stretched out my feet, have torn through the delusion of self (*tamokkhandhaṃ padāliyā*).

It appears that Uttamā had ordained and was meditating, but to no avail. She was getting nowhere. She had an interview with an elder nun who gave her classic instructions from the Buddha. Uttamā practiced diligently, not moving for seven days (a classical formula for a duration of time). On the eighth, she was enlightened.

The classical teachings on the aggregates, the six senses, and the elements (khandhāyatanadhātuyo) that Uttamā practiced are still relevant today. However, since they refer to concepts unfamiliar to most Westerners, if we are to understand how they are liberating it is worth understanding how these are understood in Buddhism.

Fundamental to what we learn by practicing with these three topics for mindfulness—the aggregates, the sense bases, and the elements—are the lessons of suffering, impermanence, and not-self. That is—by practicing with these three concepts we are able to see where we cling and to reap the fruits of letting go.

The Aggregates (Khandha)

The first of this long, compound word that Uttamā uses, khandhāyatanadhātuyo, is the Pāli term khandhas, a word literally meaning "piles" or "bundles." Throughout the Therīgāthā we read very moving stanzas in which the nuns become freed after learning about the khandhas—the five aggregates of clinging.

In his very first teaching, Dhammacakkappavattana Sutta, known as Setting in Motion the Wheel of Dhamma, the Buddha tells his disciples that he awakened to the cause of all suffering: the aggregates of clinging.

Birth is suffering, aging is suffering, sickness is suffering, death is suffering, sorrow and lamentation, pain, grief and despair are suffering; association with the loathed is suffering, dissociation from the loved is suffering, not to get what one wants is suffering. In short, *the five clinging-aggregates are suffering*. (SN 56.11)

The aggregates of clinging describe the psychophysical ways we sense, feel, perceive, and construct our worlds. We often hear them defined in the *Pāli* language as the five *khandhas*, which includes *rūpa* (form), *vedanā* (feeling), *saññā* (perception), *saṅkhāra* (mental formations), *viññāṇa* (consciousness), and the Buddha taught that suffering arises when we identify with, and cling to, any of these five. When we cling to the *khandhas*, we construct an identity bound to the past, projected into the future, and clinging to present.

Just as the nuns of the *Therīgāthā* were taught by female companions on the path ("a nun who I trusted"), we are fortunate to have well-practiced women to learn from. Upasika Kee Nanayon, considered by many to be the foremost female teacher in Thailand, instructs us on the aggregates in her 1970 *Dhamma* talk, *Training for Liberation*:

> When we understand this arising and ceasing—by turning to examine such conditions inside one's self—we will realize that it's neither something good nor bad. It is just a natural process of arising, persisting and ceasing. Try to penetrate and see this. The regular cleansing of the mind will show up any impurity, like dirt in an otherwise tidy room. Each moment you should clean out any attachment. Whatever should arise, persist and then cease—don't grasp and hold onto it! Take this principle of 'not

wanting, not grasping' deeply to heart, for then the mind will be undisturbed and free. This is such a worthwhile realization. It doesn't involve extensive knowledge—we just penetrate to see the impermanence in form, feeling, perception, conditions [mental formations] and consciousness (www.accesstoinsight.org, hereafter ATI).

The well-known German nun, Ayya Khema, addresses the suffering caused by clinging to the *khandhas* in her 1994 *Dhamma* talk, *Meditating on Not-Self,*

Take the four parts of the *khandhas* that belong to the mind apart. When we do that while it is happening—not now when we are thinking about that—but while it is happening, then we get an inkling that this isn't really *me*, that these are phenomena that are arising, which stay a moment, and then cease. How long does mind-consciousness stay on one object? And how long do thoughts last? And have we really invited them? (ATI).

The Senses (*āyatana*)

The second practice that the nun taught Uttamā was mindfulness of the senses. It is through the six senses that we know the world. This includes the five senses we commonly know with addition of the mind. The sense doors, the sense objects, and consciousness are included in the Buddhist concept of the senses as a site of clinging. In *Awake and Aware*, Ayya Khema teaches us,

Our inner being manifests in feeling, which arises through our sense contacts. Thinking is also a sense contact. Unwholesome thinking produces unpleasant feelings, such as being ill at ease, or unhappy. Seeing, hearing, tasting, touching, smelling are the five outer senses. Thinking is the inner one. All of them make contact and produce a feeling. There is the eye and the eye object. When both are in good condition, the eye consciousness arises and seeing results. The sense base, the sense object and the sense consciousness meet. When we know how this being, which we call "me," operates, we can stop the pre-programmed print-out, that's always answering the same way (ATI).

By carefully observing our sense doors coming into contact with sense objects, we notice how we become entangled in the cycle of dependent co-arising. In her essay, *Investigation for Insight*, *vipassanā* practitioner Susan Elbaum Jootla helps us understand how we, like Uttamā, can apply an investigation into the six senses to our daily practice. She includes a quote from the Buddha when she writes:

> Thus every consciousness is eye-consciousness, or ear-consciousness, or nose- or tongue- or body- or mind-consciousness, depending on which sense organ at that instant has met its object. The cycle of causality continues on from there: "Owing to eye and objects arises eye-consciousness. The coming together of the three is contact. Dependent on contact is feeling. Dependent on feeling is craving... grasping... becoming. Dependent on becoming is rebirth, decay and death, sorrow and grief... This is the arising of the world." (*SN* 12.2) From thus analyzing the genesis of existence (the "world") and of *dukkha* (as it is more often formulated) we can understand the absolutely impersonal nature of the arising of consciousness, as well as the germinal role

in creating *saṅkhāras* [mental formations] played by the internal and external sense bases (ATI).

The Elements (Dhātu)

Finally, in that long compounded word that Uttamā uses to describe what she was taught, we come to the word for elements—*dhātu*. Some of us have heard discourses on the four elements, earth, water, fire, and air, and it is easy to grasp that our world is created by these elements. In *The Meditative Mind*, Ayya Khema instructs us to note that,

> We can use mindfulness to observe that everything in existence consists of the four elements, earth, fire, water, air; and then check out what is the difference between ourselves and all else. When we take practice seriously and look at all life in such a way, then we find the truth all around as well as within us. Nothing else exists (ATI).

Pāli scholar Lily de Silva illustrates the point that elements themselves are conditions that arise out of conditions. In her 1987 piece, *The Buddhist Attitude Towards Nature,* she writes,

> Though we use a noun called "rain" which appears to denote a "thing," rain is nothing but the process of drops of water falling from the skies. Apart from this process, the activity of raining, there is no rain as such which could be expressed by a seemingly static nominal concept. The very elements of solidity *(pathavī)*, liquidity *(āpo)*, heat *(tejo)*, and mobility *(vāyo)*, recognized as the building material of nature, are all ever-changing phenomena. Even the most solid looking mountains and the very earth that supports everything on it are not beyond this inexorable law of change (ATI).

From these few examples, we get a sense of the possibilities of practicing with these objects of meditation: the aggregates, the sense bases, and the four material elements. In fact, these objects of meditation are ways to conceptualize the processes that constitute a human being. While they are sometimes taught as separate practices, classically they work together, or perhaps it's better to say that they are overlapping processes. For example, in the *Saṃyutta Nikāya*, the Bhikkhunī Vajirā describes herself as "heap of mere formations" and explains with the metaphor of a chariot:

> Just as, with an assemblage of parts,
> The word 'chariot' is used,
> So, when the aggregates exist,
> There is a convention 'a being'
> (I.553)

In addition to studying the aggregates that form the "convention known as a being," we can flesh out Vajirā's metaphor by adding that we can only experience our "being" through the interrelation of the four material elements, as well as the site of the six sense doors and their contact with the external world. While these three can help us understand the Buddha's teaching on dependent co-arising, for the purposes of this short essay it's enough to point out that whatever object of meditation a practitioner uses, the goal is the liberating insight that all things arise out of conditions, are impermanent, unsatisfactory and not personal.

Uttamā's practice and the goal of her practice can be the same for us today. Similarly, the teachings and tools given by the Buddha to the nuns have been passed down through the ages to our teachers, who continue to offer them in today's world. Just at Uttamā learned and applied what she learned from a teacher whom she trusted, we too benefit from following her example of listening and practicing.

The *Therīgāthā* provides a snapshot into the lives of these ancient nuns and tells of their devotion to practice. Their stories of liberation can be inspirations to us today, whether we are lay or ordained, men or women.

Works Cited

Gross, Rita M., *Buddhism After Patriarchy: A Feminist History, Analysis and Reconstruction of Buddhism*, SUNY 1993

Access to Insight (ATI) www.accesstoinsight.org

Nona Olivia has been a student of Buddhism and meditation practitioner for many decades. She holds a PhD from Brown University and teaches at the University of Colorado in Boulder. Her area of expertise is the role of women in ancient religious traditions.

The Buddha via the Bible

How Western Buddhists Read the Pāli Canon

VEN. THANISSARO BHIKKHU

WESTERN CULTURE learned how to read spiritual texts by reading the Bible. Not that we all read it the same way—quite the contrary. We've fought long, bloody wars over the issue. But most of the differences in our readings lie within a fairly tight constellation of ideas about authority and obligation, meaning and mystery, and the purpose of history and time. And even though those ideas grew from the peculiarities of the Bible and of Western history, we regard them as perfectly natural, and in some cases, even better than natural: modern. They're so implicit in our mindset that when people rebel against the Bible's authority, their notions of rebellion and authority often derive from the tradition they're trying to reject.

So it's only to be expected that when we encounter spiritual texts from other traditions, we approach them as we would the Bible. And because this tendency is so ingrained, we rarely realize what we've done.

For example, the way we read the *Pāli* Canon has largely been influenced by modern attitudes toward the Bible that date back to the German Romantics and American Transcendentalists—primarily Ralph Waldo Emerson. Even though we seldom read these thinkers outside of literature or history classes, their ideas permeate our culture through their influence on humanistic psychology, liberal spirituality, and the study of comparative religion: portals through which many of us first encounter the religions of other cultures. The question is, Do these ideas do justice to the *Pāli* Canon? Are we getting the most out of the Canon if we read it this way? We rarely ask these questions because our reading habits are invisible to us. We need fresh eyes to see how odd those habits are. And a good way to freshen our eyes is to look historically at the particulars of where these habits come from, and the unspoken assumptions behind them.

The Romantics and Transcendentalists formulated their ideas about reading the Bible in response to developments in linguistics, psychology, and historical scholarship in the 17th to 19th centuries. This is what makes them modern. They were addressing a culture that had grown skeptical toward organized religion and had embraced intellectual principles capable of challenging the Bible's authority. Thus, to be taken seriously, they had to speak the language of universal historical and psychological laws. However, the actual content of those laws drew on ideas dating back through the Middle Ages to the Church Fathers—and even further, to the Bible itself: doctrines such as Paul's dictum that the invisible things of God are clearly seen through the visible things He made; Augustine's teaching on Christ the Inner Teacher, illuminating the mind; and John Cassian's instructions on how to read the Bible metaphorically. So even though the Romantic/Transcendentalist view is modern and universal in its form, its actual substance is largely ancient and specific to the West.

In the complete version of this article—available at www.Dhammatalks.org—I've traced how these ideas were shaped by developments in Western history. Here, however, I want to focus on the parallels between the psychological laws the Transcendentalists formulated for reading the Bible, and the assumptions that modern Dharma teachers bring to reading the *Pāli* Canon. My purpose is to show that, while these assumptions seem natural and universal to us, they are culturally limited and limiting: ill-suited for getting the most out of what the Canon provides.

THE TRANSCENDENTALIST APPROACH to the Bible boils down to eight principles. The first principle concerns the nature of the universe; the second, the means by which the human mind can best connect with that nature; and the remaining six, the implications of the first two concerning how the Bible should be read. In the following discussion, the quotations illustrating each principle are from Emerson.

1. The universe is an organic whole composed of vital forces. (The technical term for this view is "monistic vitalism.") This whole is essentially good because it is continuously impelled forward by the over-arching force of a benevolent creator—which Emerson called the Over-soul—operating both in external nature and in the inner recesses of the soul. People suffer because their social conditioning estranges them from the inner and outer influences of the Over-soul, depriving them of its sustaining, creative power. Thus the spiritual life is essentially a search for oneness with the whole.

The simplest person, who in his integrity worships God, becomes God... the heart in thee is the heart of all; not a valve, not a wall, not an intersection is there anywhere in nature, but one blood rolls uninterruptedly in endless circulation through all men, as the water of the globe is all one sea, and, truly seen, its tide is one.

2. This sense of oneness is best found by adopting a receptive, open attitude toward the influences of nature on a sensory, pre-verbal level.

Standing on the bare ground,—my head bathed by the blithe air, and uplifted into infinite space,—all mean egotism vanishes. I become a transparent eye-ball; I am nothing; I see all; the currents of the Universal Being circulate through me; I am part or particle of God.

3. The Bible can comfort the soul estranged from nature, but it should not be granted absolute authority because the inspiration it records is only second-hand, interfering with the soul's direct contact with the One.

The relations of the soul to the divine spirit are so pure that it is profane to seek to interpose helps.

The saints and demigods whom history worships we are constrained to accept with a grain of allowance. Though in our lonely hours we draw a new strength out of their memory, yet, pressed on our attention, as they are by the thoughtless and customary, they fatigue and invade. The soul gives itself, alone, original, and pure, to the Lonely, Original, and Pure, who, on that condition, gladly inhabits, leads, and speaks through it.

4. The Bible's message is also limited in that it was composed for a less enlightened stage in human history.

If, therefore, a man claims to know and speak of God, and carries you backward to the phraseology of some old mouldered nation in another country, in another world, believe him not. Is the acorn better than the oak which is its fullness and completion? Is the parent better than the child into whom he has cast his ripened being? Whence, then, this worship of the past? The centuries are conspirators against the sanity and authority of the soul.

The idealism of Jesus... is a crude statement of the fact that all nature is the rapid efflux of goodness executing and organizing itself.

5. The Bible's authority is actually dangerous in that it stifles the soul's creative impulses, the most direct experience of the Over-soul's vital force within.

The one thing in the world, of value, is the active soul... The soul active sees absolute truth and utters truth, or creates.

When we have broken our god of tradition, and ceased from our god of rhetoric, then may God fire the heart with his presence.

What is that abridgement and selection we observe in all spiritual activity, but itself the creative impulse?

Yet see what strong intellects dare not yet hear God himself, unless he speak the phraseology of I know not what David, or Jeremiah, or Paul... When we have new perception, we shall gladly disburden the memory of its hoarded treasures as old rubbish.

6. Another limitation on the language of the Bible is that it is expressive rather than descriptive. In other words, unlike the meta-cultural laws of psychology, it does not describe universal human truths. Instead, it expresses through metaphor how the force of the Over-soul felt to particular people at particular times. Thus, to be relevant to the present, it is best read, not as a scholar would—trying to find what actually happened in the past, or what it meant to its authors—but as a poet might read the poetry of others, judging for him or herself what metaphors will be most useful for inspiring his or her own creative genius.

[One] must attain and maintain that lofty sight where poetry and annals are alike.

The Garden of Eden, the sun standing still in Gibeon, is poetry thenceforward to all nations. Who cares what the fact was, when we have made a constellation of it to hang in heaven as an immortal sign.

In the book I read, the good thought returns to me, as every truth will, the image of the whole soul. To the bad thought which I find in it, the same soul becomes a discerning, separating sword, and lops it away.

7. By reading the Bible creatively in this way, one is assisting in the progress of God's will in the world.

Because the soul is progressive, it never quite repeats itself, but in every act attempts the production of a new and fairer whole.... We need not fear that we can lose any thing by the progress of the soul. The soul may be trusted to the end.

8. The Transcendentalists all agreed with the Romantics that the soul's most trustworthy sense of morality came from a sense of interconnectedness within oneself and with others. They differed among themselves, though, in how this interconnectedness was best embodied. Emerson advocated focusing on the present-moment particulars of one's ordinary activities. In his words, *"The invariable mark of wisdom is to see the miraculous in the common."*

Other Transcendentalists, however—such as Orestes Brownson, Margaret Fuller, and Theodore Parker—insisted that true inner oneness was impossible in a society rent by injustice and inequality. Thus, they advocated reading the Bible prophetically, as God's call to engage in progressive social work. Emerson, in turn, retorted that unless change came first from within, even the ideal social structure would be corrupted by the lack of inner contact with God. Thus the two camps reached a standoff.

Still, even the socially engaged Transcendentalists read the Bible creatively and metaphorically, seeking not its original message but a new message appropriate for modern needs. Brownson, for instance, followed the French socialist, Pierre Leroux, in interpreting the Last Supper as Jesus' call to all Christians to drop artificial social divisions caused by wage labor, capitalist exploitation, external signs of status, etc., and to construct a new social system that would allow all humanity to celebrate their mutual interconnectedness.

HISTORIANS HAVE TRACED how these eight principles—including the split in the eighth—have shaped American liberal spirituality in Christian, Reform Jewish, and New Age circles up to the present. Emerson's way of phrasing these points may sound quaint, but the underlying principles are still familiar even to those who've never read him. Thus it's only natural that Americans raised in these traditions, on coming to Buddhism, would bring these principles along. Emerson himself, in his later years, led the way in this direction through his selective appreciation of Hindu and Buddhist teachings—which he tended to conflate—and modern Western Buddhist teachers still apply all eight principles to the *Pāli* Canon even today.

In the following discussion I've illustrated these principles, as applied to the Canon, with quotations from both lay and monastic teachers. The teachers are left unnamed because I want to focus, not on individuals, but on what historians call a cultural syndrome, in which both the teachers and their audiences share responsibility for influencing one another: the teachers, by how they try to explain and persuade; the audiences, by what they're inclined to accept or reject. Some of the teachers quoted here embrace Romantic/Transcendentalist ideas more fully than others, but the tendency is present, at least to some extent, in them all.

1. The first principle is that the Canon, like all spiritual texts, takes interconnectedness—the experience of unity within and without—as its basic theme. On attaining this unity, one drops the identity of one's small self and embraces a new identity with the universe at large.

The goal [of Dhamma practice] is integration, through love and acceptance, openness and receptivity, leading to a unified wholeness of experience without the artificial boundaries of separate selfhood.

It is the goal of spiritual life to open to the reality that exists beyond our small sense of self. Through the gate of oneness we awaken to the ocean within us, we come to know in yet another way that the seas we swim in are not separate from all that lives. When our identity expands to include everything, we find a peace with the dance of the world. It is all ours, and our heart is full and empty, large enough to embrace it all.

2. The Canon's prime contribution to human spirituality is its insight into how interconnectedness can be cultivated through systematic training in mindfulness, defined as an open, receptive, pre-verbal awareness. This provides a practical technique for fostering the sort of transparent religious consciousness that Emerson extolled. One teacher, in fact, describes mindfulness as "sacred awareness."

Mindfulness is presence of mind, attentiveness or awareness. Yet the kind of awareness involved in mindfulness differs profoundly from the kind of awareness at work in our usual mode of consciousness... The mind is deliberately kept at the level of bare attention, a detached observation of what is happening within us and around us in the present moment. In the practice of right mindfulness the mind is trained to remain in the present, open, quiet, and alert, contemplating the present event. All judgements and interpretations have to be suspended, or if they occur, just registered and dropped. The task is simply to note whatever comes up just as it is occurring, riding the changes of events in the way a surfer rides the waves on the sea.

3. However, the Canon does not speak with final authority on how this receptive state should be used or how life should be led. This is because the nature of spiritual inspiration is purely individual and mysterious. Where the Transcendentalists spoke of following the soul, Western Buddhists speak of following the heart. As one teacher, who has stated that following one's heart might mean taking the path of psychotropic drugs, has said:

No one can define for us exactly what our path should be.

[A]ll the teachings of books, maps, and beliefs have little to do with wisdom or compassion. At best they are a signpost, a finger pointing at the moon, or the leftover dialogue from a time when someone received some true spiritual nourishment.... We must discover within ourselves our own way to become conscious, to live a life of the spirit.

Religion and philosophy have their value, but in the end all we can do is open to mystery.

4. The Canon's authority is also limited by the cultural circumstances in which it was composed. Several teachers, for example, have recommended dropping the Canon's teachings on kamma because they were simply borrowed from the cultural presuppositions of the Buddha's time:

Even the most creative, world-transforming individuals cannot stand on their own shoulders. They too remain dependent upon their cultural context, whether intellectual or spiritual—which is precisely what Buddhism's emphasis on impermanence and causal interdependence implies. The Buddha also expressed his new, liberating insight in the only way he could, using the religious categories that his culture could understand. Inevitably, then, his way of expressing the Dhamma was a blend of the truly new... and the conventional religious thought of his time. Although the new transcends the conventional... the new cannot immediately and completely escape the conventional wisdom it surpasses.

5. Another reason to restrict the Canon's authority is that its teachings can harm the sensitive psyche. Where Emerson warned against allowing the Bible to stifle individual creativity, Western Buddhists warn that the Canon's talk of eliminating greed, aversion, and delusion ignores, in an unhealthy way, the realities of the human dimension.

If you go into ancient Indian philosophy, there is a great emphasis on perfection as the absolute, as the ideal. [But] is that archetype, is that ideal, what we actually experience?

The images we have been taught about perfection can be destructive to us. Instead of clinging to an inflated, superhuman view of perfection, we learn to allow ourselves the space of kindness.

6. Because the language of the Canon is archetypal, it should be read, not as descriptive, but as expressive and poetic. And that expression is best absorbed intuitively.

It's never a matter of trying to figure it all out, rather we pick up these phrases and chew them over, taste them, digest them and let them energize us by virtue of their own nature.

Even these ostensibly literal maps may be better read as if they were a kind of poem, rich in possible meanings.

7. To read the Canon as poetry may yield new meanings unintended by the compilers, but that simply advances a process at work throughout Buddhist history. Some thinkers have explained this process as a form of vitalism, with Buddhism or the Dharma identified as the vital force. Sometimes the vitalism is explicit—as when one thinker defined Buddhism as "an inexpressible living force." At other times, it is no less present for being implied:

The great strength of Buddhism throughout its history is that it has succeeded many times in reinventing itself according to the needs of its new host culture. What is happening today in the West is no different.

In each historical period, the Dharma finds new means to unfold its potential in ways precisely linked to that era's distinctive conditions. Our own era provides the appropriate stage for the transcendent truth of the Dharma to bend back upon the world and engage human suffering at multiple levels, not in mere contemplation but in effective, relief-granting action.

8. As this last quotation shows, some thinkers recommend reading the Canon not only poetically but also prophetically as a source of moral imperatives for social action in our times. Because the Canon says little on the topic of social action, this requires a creative approach to the text.

We can root out thematically relevant Buddhist themes, texts, and archetypes and clarify them as core teachings for Buddhist based social change work.

Of the various themes found in the *Pāli* Canon, dependent co-arising—interpreted as interconnectedness—is most commonly cited as a source for social obligation, paralleling the way the Transcendentalists saw interconnectedness as the source of all moral feeling.

Numerous thinkers have hailed this prophetic reading of the Canon as a new turning of the *Dhamma* wheel, in which the *Dhamma* grows by absorbing advances in modern Western culture. Many are the lessons, they say, that the *Dhamma* must learn from the West, among them: democracy, equality, Gandhian nonviolence, humanistic psychology, ecofeminism, sustainable economics, systems theory, deep ecology, new paradigm science, and the Christian and Jewish examples of religious social action. We are assured that these developments are positive because the deepest forces of reality—within and without—can be trusted to the end.

We must be open to a variety of responses toward social change that come from no particular "authority" but are grounded in the radical creativity that comes when concepts fall away.

There is an underlying unity to all things, and a wise heart knows this as it knows the in-and-out of the breath. They are all part of a sacred whole in which we exist, and in the deepest way they are completely trustworthy. We need not fear the energies of this world or any other.

Often the trustworthiness of the mind is justified with a teaching drawn from the Mahayana: the principle of Buddha-nature present in all. This principle has no basis in the *Pāli* Canon, and so its adoption in Western *Theravāda* is frequently attributed to the popularity of Mahayana in Western Buddhism at large. Only rarely is the question asked, Why do Westerners find the Mahayana attractive? Is it because the Mahayana teaches doctrines we're already predisposed to accept? Probably so—especially when you consider that although the principle of Buddha-nature is interpreted in many ways within the Mahayana itself, here in the West it's primarily understood in the form closest to the Transcendentalist idea of innate goodness.

Compassion is our deepest nature. It arises from our interconnection with all things.

THESE EIGHT PRINCIPLES for interpreting the *Pāli* Canon are often presented as meta-cultural truths but, as we have seen, they developed in the specific context of the Western engagement with the Bible. In other words, they're historically conditioned. When we compare them to the Canon itself, we find that they directly contradict the *Dhamma*. At the same time, when teachers try to justify these principles on the basis of the Canon, we find that they're invariably misreading the text.

1. The idea that spiritual life is a search for unity depends on the assumption that the universe is an organic whole, and that the whole is essentially good. The Canon, however, consistently portrays the goal of the spiritual life as transcendence: The world—which is synonymous with the All (SN 35:23)—is a dangerous river

over which one has to cross to safety on the other side. The state of oneness or non-duality is conditioned (AN 10:29): still immersed in the river, unsafe. In reaching nibbana, one is not returning to the source of things (MN 1), but reaching something never reached before (AN 5:77): a dimension beyond all space and time. And in attaining this dimension, one is not establishing a new identity, for all identities—even infinite ones (DN 15)—ultimately prevent that attainment, and so have to be dropped.

2. The Canon never defines mindfulness as an open, receptive, pre-verbal state. In fact, its standard definition for the faculty of mindfulness is the ability to keep things in mind (SN 48:9). Thus, in the practice of right mindfulness, one is keeping one of four frames of reference in mind: body, feelings, mind, and mental qualities, remembering to stay with these things in and of themselves. And some of the more vivid analogies for the practice of mindfulness suggest anything but an open, receptive, non-judging state.

> "Just as when a person whose turban or head was on fire would put forth extra desire, effort, diligence, endeavor, earnestness, mindfulness, and alertness to put out the fire on his turban or head; in the same way, the monk should put forth extra desire... mindfulness, and alertness for the abandoning of those evil, unskillful mental qualities." — *AN 10:51*

> "Suppose, monks, that a large crowd of people comes thronging together, saying, 'The beauty queen! The beauty queen!' And suppose that the beauty queen is highly accomplished at singing and dancing, so that an even greater crowd comes thronging, saying, 'The beauty queen is singing! The beauty queen is dancing!' Then a man comes along, desiring life and shrinking from death, desiring pleasure and abhorring pain. They say to him, 'Now look here, mister. You

must take this bowl filled to the brim with oil and carry it on your head in between the great crowd and the beauty queen. A man with a raised sword will follow right behind you, and wherever you spill even a drop of oil, right there will he cut off your head.' Now what do you think, monks? Will that man, not paying attention to the bowl of oil, let himself get distracted outside?"

"No, lord."

"I have given you this parable to convey a meaning. The meaning is this: The bowl filled to the brim with oil stands for mindfulness immersed in the body." — *SN 47:20*

There's a tendency, even among serious scholars, to mine in the Canon for passages presenting a more spacious, receptive picture of mindfulness. But this tendency, in addition to ignoring the basic definition of mindfulness, denies the essential unity among the factors of the path—one such scholar, to make his case, had to define right mindfulness and right effort as two mutually exclusive forms of practice. This suggests that the tendency to define mindfulness as an open, receptive, non-judging state comes from a source other than the Canon. It's possible to find Asian roots for this tendency, in the schools of meditation that define mindfulness as bare awareness or mere noting. But the way the West has morphed these concepts in the direction of acceptance and affirmation has less to do with Asian tradition, and more to do with our cultural tendency to exalt a pre-verbal receptivity as the source for spiritual inspiration.

3. The Canon states clearly that there is only one path to nibbana (DN 16). Trying to find awakening in ways apart from the noble eightfold path is like trying to squeeze oil from gravel, or milking a cow by twisting its horn (MN 126). The Buddha's knowledge of the way to awakening is like that of an expert

gatekeeper who knows, after encircling the walls of a city, that there's only one way into the city: the gate he guards (AN 10:95).

One of the tests for determining whether one has reached the first level of awakening is if, on reflection, one realizes that no one outside the Buddha's teaching teaches the true, accurate, way to the goal (SN 48:53). Although individual people may have to focus on issues particular to their temperament, the basic outline of the path is the same for all.

4. Obviously the Buddha's language and metaphors were culturally conditioned, but it's hard to identify any of his essential teachings as limited in that way. He claimed a knowledge of the past that far outstrips ours (DN 29; DN1), and he'd often claim direct knowledge when stating that he was speaking for the past, present, and future when describing, for instance, how physical, verbal, and mental actions are to be purified (MN 61) and the highest emptiness that can be attained (MN 121). This is why the *Dhamma* is said to be timeless, and why the first level of awakening verifies that this is so.

At the same time, when people speak of essential Buddhist teachings that are limited by the cultural conventions of the Buddha's time, they're usually misinformed as to what those conventions were. For instance, with the doctrine of kamma: Even though the Buddha used the word *kamma* like his contemporaries, his conception of what kamma was and how it worked differed radically from theirs (AN 3:62; MN 101).

5. Similarly, people who describe the dangers of following a particular Buddhist teaching usually deal in caricatures. For instance, one teacher who warns of the dangers of the linear path to attainment describes that path as follows:

The linear path holds up an idealistic vision of the perfected human, a Buddha or saint or sage. In this vision, all greed, anger, fear, judgment, delusion, personal ego, and desire are uprooted forever, completely eliminated. What is left is an absolutely unwavering, radiant, pure human being who never experiences any difficulties, an illuminated sage who follows only the Tao or God's will and never his or her own.

Although this may be a possible vision of the linear path, it differs in many crucial details from the vision offered in the Canon. The Buddha certainly passed judgment on people and taught clear criteria for what are and are not valid grounds for judgment (AN 7:64; AN 4:192; MN 110). He experienced difficulties in setting up the monastic *Sangha*. But that does not invalidate the fact that his greed, aversion, and delusion were gone.

As MN 22 states, there are dangers in grasping the *Dhamma* wrongly. In the context of that discourse, the Buddha is referring to people who grasp the *Dhamma* for the sake of argument; at present we might point out the dangers in grasping the teachings neurotically. But there are even greater dangers in misrepresenting the teachings, or in dragging them down to our own level, rather than using them to lift ourselves up. As the Buddha said, people who claim that he said what he didn't say, or didn't say what he did, are slandering him (AN 2:23). In doing so, they blind themselves to the *Dhamma*.

6. Although the Canon contains a few passages where the Buddha and his awakened disciples speak poetically and expressively of their attainment, those passages are rare. Far more common are the descriptive passages, in which the Buddha tells explicitly how to get to awakening. As he said in a famous simile, the knowledge gained in his awakening was like the leaves in the forest; the knowledge he taught, like the leaves in his hand (SN 56:31). And he chose those particular leaves because they served a purpose, helping others develop the skills needed for release. This

point is supported by the imagery and analogies employed throughout the Canon. Although some of the more poetic passages draw images from nature, they are greatly outnumbered by analogies drawn from physical skills—cooking, farming, archery, carpentry—making the point that *Dhamma* practice is a skill that can be understood and mastered in ways similar to more ordinary skills.

The Buddha's descriptions of the path are phrased primarily in psychological terms—just like the meta-cultural principles of the Transcendentalists and Romantics. Obviously, the Canon's maps of mental processes differ from those proposed by Western psychology, but that doesn't invalidate them. They were drawn for a particular purpose—to help attain the end of suffering—and they have to be tested fairly, not against our preferences, but against their ability to perform their intended function.

The poetic approach to the Canon overlooks the care with which the Buddha tried to make his instructions specific and clear. As he once commented (AN 2:46), there are two types of assemblies: those trained in bombast, and those trained in cross-questioning. In the former, the students are taught "literary works—the works of poets, artful in sound, artful in expression, the work of outsiders" and are not encouraged to pin down what the meaning of those beautiful words might be. In the latter—and here the Buddha was describing his own method of teaching—the students are taught the *Dhamma* and "when they have mastered that *Dhamma*, they cross-question one another about it and dissect it: 'How is this? What is the meaning of this?' They make open what isn't open, make plain what isn't plain, dispel doubt on its various doubtful points." To treat such teachings as poetry distorts how and why they were taught.

7. A vitalist interpretation of Buddhist history does a disservice both to the Buddha's teachings and to historical truth. To begin with, the Canon does not portray history as purposeful. Time moves in cycles, but those movements mean nothing. This is why the Buddha used the term *samsara*—"wandering-on"—to describe the course of beings through time. Only if we decide to end this wandering will our lives develop purpose and direction. Otherwise, our course is aimless:

> "Just as a stick thrown up in the air lands sometimes on its base, sometimes on its side, sometimes on its tip; in the same way, beings hindered by ignorance and fettered by craving, transmigrating and wandering on, sometimes go from this world to another world, sometimes come from another world to this." — *SN 15:9*

Second, Buddhism does not have a will. It does not adapt; people adapt Buddhism to their various ends. And because the adapters are not always wise, there's no guarantee that the adaptations are skillful. Just because other people have made changes in the *Dhamma* doesn't automatically justify the changes we want to make. Think, for instance, of how some Mahayana traditions dropped the Vinaya's procedures for dealing with teacher-student sexual abuse: Was this the *Dhamma* wisely adapting itself to their needs?

The Buddha foresaw that people would introduce what he called "synthetic *Dhamma*"—and when that happened, he said, the true *Dhamma* would disappear (SN 16:13). He compared the process to what happens when a wooden drum develops a crack, into which a peg is inserted, and then another crack, into which another peg is inserted, and so on until nothing is left of the original drum-body. All that remains is a mass of pegs, which cannot come near to producing the sound of the original drum (SN 20:7).

Some scholars have found the Canon's warnings about the decay of the *Dhamma* ironic.

This strongly held view [that Buddhism should not change] seems a bit odd in a religion that also teaches that resistance to all-pervasive change is a root cause of misery.

The Buddha, however, didn't embrace change, didn't encourage change for the sake of change, and certainly didn't define resistance to change as the cause of suffering. Suffering is caused by *identifying* with change or with things that change. Many are the discourses describing the perils of "going along with the flow" in terms of a river that can carry one to whirlpools, monsters, and demons (Iti 109). And as we noted above, a pervasive theme in the Canon is that true happiness is found only when one crosses over the river to the other side.

8. The Buddha was not a prophet, and he did not pretend to speak for God. Thus he was careful never to present his teachings as moral obligations. His *shoulds* were all conditional. As the first line of the Karaṇīya Mettā Sutta (Khp 9) states,

> This is to be done by one skilled in aims
> who wants to break through to the state of peace;

In other words, *if* you want to break through to a state of peace, *then* this is what you have to do. And although generosity is one of the things one must do to attain that goal, when the Buddha was asked where a gift should be given (SN 3:24), he responded, "Wherever the mind feels confidence." This means that if we regard social action as a gift, there is no need to seek the Buddha's sanction for feeling inspired to give in that way; we can just go ahead and do it—as long as our actions conform with the precepts. But it also means that we cannot use his words to impose a sense of obligation on others that they should give in the same way.

This is especially true in a teaching like the Buddha's, which is strongly pragmatic, with each teaching focused on a particular end. To take those teachings out of context, applying them to other ends, distorts them. The teaching on dependent co-arising, which is often interpreted as the Canon's version of interconnectedness, is a case in point. The factors in dependent co-arising are primarily internal, dealing with the psychology of suffering, and are aimed at showing how knowledge of the four noble truths can be applied to bring suffering to an end. There is nothing to celebrate in the way the ordinary interaction of these factors leads to suffering. To turn this teaching into a celebration of the interconnectedness of the universe, or as a guide to the moral imperative of social action, is to thwart its purpose and to open it to ridicule from people disinclined to accept its moral authority over their lives.

At the same time, the Canon questions the underlying assumption—which we've inherited not only from the Transcendentalists and Romantics, but also from their Enlightenment forebears—that human culture is evolving ever upwards. The early discourses present the opposite picture, that human life is getting worse as a sphere for *Dhamma* practice, and it's easy to point out features of modern life that confirm this picture. To begin with, *Dhamma* practice is a skill, requiring the attitudes and mental abilities developed by physical skills, and yet we are a society whose physical skills are fast eroding away. Thus the mental virtues nurtured by physical skills have atrophied. At the same time, the social hierarchy required by skills—in which students apprentice themselves to a master—has mostly disappeared, so we've unlearned the attitudes needed to live in hierarchy in a healthy and productive way. We like to think that we're shaping the *Dhamma* with our highest cultural ideals, but some of our lower ways are actually dominating the shape of Western *Dhamma:* The sense of neurotic entitlement produced by the culture of consumerism is a case in point, as are the hype of the mass media and the demands of the mass-market for a *Dhamma* that sells.

As for trusting the impulses of the mind: Try a thought experiment and take the above quote—that we must be open to the radical creativity that comes when concepts fall away—and imagine how it would sound in different contexts. Coming from a socially concerned Buddhist activist, it might not seem disconcerting. But coming from a rebel leader teaching child-soldiers in a civil-war torn country, or a greedy financier contemplating new financial instruments, it would be a cause for alarm.

The Buddha probably would have agreed with the Romantics and Transcendentalists that the human mind is essentially active in making sense of its surroundings. But he would have differed with their estimation that this activity is, at its root, divinely inspired. In his analysis of dependent co-arising, mental fabrication comes from ignorance (SN 12:2); the way to end suffering is to end that fabrication; and this requires an attitude, not of trust, but of heedful vigilance (DN 16). Thus heedfulness must extend both to one's attitude toward one's intuitions and to the ways with which one reads the Canon.

THIS POINT TOUCHES on what is probably the most central issue in why the Transcendentalist approach to reading the Bible is inappropriate for reading the *Pāli* Canon: the issue of authority. In the Bible, God's authority is absolute because He is the creator of all. We, having been created for His inscrutable ends, must trust His authority absolutely. Although the Transcendentalists denied that the Bible carried God's absolute authority, they did not deny the concept of absolute authority in and of itself; they simply moved it from the Bible and, bypassing other alternatives, placed it with the spontaneous intuitions of the heart. Following their lead, we as a culture tend to see the issue of authority as a simple either/or: either absolutely in the Bible or absolutely in our intuitions. As a result, when we read in the Kalama Sutta (AN 3:65), "Don't go by reports, by legends, by traditions, by scripture... or by the thought, 'This contemplative is our teacher,'" we skip over the words in the ellipsis and assume that there is only one other alternative, as stated in a message rubber-stamped on the back of an envelope I once received: *"Follow your own sense of right and wrong—The Buddha."*

However, the words in the ellipsis are equally important: "Don't go by logical conjecture, by inference, by analogies, by agreement through pondering views, or by probability." In other words, you can't go simply by what seems reasonable or agreeable to you. You can't go simply by your intuitions. Instead, the Buddha recommends that you test a particular teaching from a variety of angles: Is it skillful? Is it blameless? Is it praised or criticized by the wise? When put into practice does it lead to harm and suffering, or to wellbeing and happiness?

This requires approaching the practice as a skill to be mastered, one that has already been mastered by the wise. Although a part of mastery is learning to gauge the results of your actions, that's not the whole story. You must learn how to tap into the wisdom and experience of experts, and learn to gauge the results of your actions—at the very least—against standards they have set. This is why we read and study the Canon: to gain a clear understanding of what the wise have discovered, to open our minds to the questions they found fruitful, so that we can apply the wisdom of their expertise as we try to develop our own.

It's in this context that we can understand the nature of the Buddha's authority as presented in the *Pāli* discourses. He speaks, not with the authority of a creator, but with the authority of an expert. Only in the Vinaya does he assume the added authority of a lawgiver. In the discourses, he calls himself a doctor; a trainer; an admirable, experienced friend who has mastered a specific skill: putting an end to suffering. He provides explicit recommendations on how to act, speak, and think to bring about that result; instructions on how to develop qualities of mind that allow you to assess your actions accurately; and questions to ask yourself in measuring your progress along the way.

It's up to us whether we want to accept or reject his expertise, but if we accept it he asks for our respect. This means, in the context of an apprentice culture—the culture set up in the Vinaya (Cv.VIII.11-12)—that you take at face value his instructions on how to end suffering and give them a serious try. Where the instructions are ambiguous, you use your ingenuity to fill in the blanks, but then you test the results against the standards the Buddha has set, making every effort to be heedful in reading accurately and fairly what you have done. This sort of test requires a serious commitment—for a sense of how serious, it's instructive to read the biographies of the Thai forest masters. And because the commitment is so serious, the Buddha advises exercising careful judgment in choosing the person to whom you apprentice yourself (AN 4:192) and tells you what to look for before growing close to a teacher (MN 95). You can't trust every teacher to be a genuinely admirable friend.

This is all very straightforward, but it requires stepping outside the limitations of our culturally conditioned ways. And again, it's up to us whether we want to read the *Pāli* Canon on its own terms. If we don't, we're free to continue reading it poetically and prophetically, taking the Buddha's instructions as grist for our own creative intuitions. But if that's our approach, we'll never be in a position to judge adequately whether his instructions for putting an end to suffering actually work.

Ven. Thanissaro Bhikkhu (Geoffrey DeGraff) is an American monk of the Thai forest tradition. After graduating from Oberlin College in 1971 with a degree in European Intellectual History, he studied meditation under Ajaan Fuang Jotiko in Thailand, himself a student of the late Ajaan Lee, and ordained in 1976. In 1991 he traveled to the hills of San Diego County, USA, where he helped establish Mettā Forest Monastery, of which he is now the abbot. He is a prolific writer and translator. Many of his works can be found online at www.accesstoinsight.org and www.Dhammatalks.org.

Getting Started with the Suttas

VEN. THANISSARO BHIKKHU

IF YOU'RE NEW to reading the collection of the Buddha's teachings, I recommend starting with two articles before plunging into the suttas. The first is "Befriending the Suttas," by John Bullitt, available on Access to Insight (as is everything else I'm recommending here; the address is www.accesstoinsight.org). This provides practical tips on attitudes and approaches to bring to the act of reading. The second article is "When You Know for Yourselves...", which cites passages from the Canon itself indicating how its compilers felt it should be read, and how the act of reading (or listening, in their day) should fit into the practice as a whole.

Next, familiarize yourself with what the suttas themselves say about basic topics. A good place to start is with *The Path to Freedom* (labeled as "self-guided tour"), which contains short passages about the Buddha, *Dhamma*, and *Sangha*. Then you might try any of the study guides on the website. I'd recommend *Recognizing the Dhamma.* This presents a list of eight principles for testing what is and isn't *Dhamma*. The first two items in the list are the most rigorous tests, so you might want to start with the last item—being unburdensome—and work backwards from there. I'd also recommend the study guide on kamma, for this topic underlies everything else.

With this background, try reading some suttas in their entirety, for the *way* the Buddha presents his teachings is an important teaching on kamma and discernment in and of itself. Among the best suttas for introducing the Buddha in action are discourses number 61, 58, 126, 27, 36, 140, and 72 from the *Majjhima Nikāya* (the Middle Length Discourses).

For a brief introduction to the intellectual context of the Buddha's time, try *Majjhima* 14 and 101, the beginning of *Dīgha Nikāya* 2, and *Aṅguttara Nikāya* 3:62.

Good suttas from the *Majjhima Nikāya* on meditation practice include, in addition to 140: 119, 118, 20, 2, and 121. This last sutta takes a pattern that the Buddha introduced to his young son, Rahula, in an everyday context in *Majjhima* 61, and applies it to advanced states of meditation: a useful reminder that the basics should not be overlooked or underestimated, for they inform the entire practice.

Studying to Go Beyond Buddhism

Translation of the Discourse on the Highest

GIL FRONSDAL

THE DISCOURSE ON THE HIGHEST is the fifth in a remarkable set of 16 discourses collectively called *The Book of Eights* (the *Aṭṭhakavagga*). Found in the larger collection of texts called the *Sutta Nipāta*, the *Book of Eights* is often considered to represent the earliest Buddhist teachings, perhaps even originating in the first years of the Buddha's 45 years as a teacher. Among the evidence suggesting its antiquity is its use of language more archaic than what is usually found in the suttas. In addition, because the *Book of Eight* is mentioned in some of the *Pāli* suttas, it must pre-date at least those suttas. An unusual feature of this collection is the absence of many of the standard descriptions of Buddhist teachings. Here, there is no mention of the Four Noble Truths, the Eightfold Path, the Four Foundations of Mindfulness, the various levels of deep concentration, the Four Stages of Awakening, the twelve-fold chain of dependent origination, as well as any role or importance for rebirth. If the *Book of Eights* does indeed represent the Buddha's earliest teachings, perhaps it comes from a time before he fully systematized and developed the core insights he had upon his Awakening.

The *Book of Eights* does not contradict the standard descriptions of Buddhist doctrine. Instead, it is instructive about how to relate to these more familiar teachings. The primary focus of the 16 suttas is non-clinging and the peace that comes from not clinging. In line with this, the *Book of Eights*, and especially in the *Discourse on the Highest*, emphasizes the importance of not clinging to spiritual doctrine, knowledge, or opinions. In other words, the goal of the Buddha's path of practice is not found in particular insights, understandings, views, practices, or ethical behavior. The goal is found in the release from clinging.

This does not mean that there are no insights and understandings to be discovered, but they are not what bring freedom. Freedom is found in letting go. It therefore means that the ultimate aim of practice is not found in Buddhist teachings and practices themselves. While these may aid in and point toward freedom, we must be careful to not be attached to the teachings and practices. I believe the *Discourse on the Highest* is meant to challenge such attachment when it says in verse 797 that a person should not depend on precepts and religious observances or practices.

One of the main forms of religious attachment is to hold one's own religion or religious views as being superior to others. The *Discourse on the Highest* begins by stressing that doing so is itself a form of attachment, here called an entanglement or knot. The attainment of freedom has nothing to do with championing one set of doctrines and practice over others.

The *Discourse on the Highest* reminds us that the goal of Buddhist practice is to go beyond Buddhism. When this is accomplished, we discover the freedom of the Buddha and so overcome any attachment to Buddhism itself.

The Discourse on the Highest

Fifth Discourse from the *Aṭṭhakavagga* of the *Sutta Nipāta*

Having views about what is "highest"
    A person makes these the best in the world
    And calls all others 'inferior."
    As such they have not gone beyond quarrelling.   796

When one sees personal advantage
    In things seen, heard, and thought out
    Or in precepts and religious observances,
    And then grasps at these,
    One sees all else as inferior.   797

What one relies on so to see all else as inferior
    Is an entanglement, say those who are skilled.
    A monastic should, therefore,
    Not depend on things seen, heard, or thought out
    Or on precepts and religious observances.   798

Nor should they make up views in the world
    By means of knowledge, precepts and religious
        observances.
    Nor should they think of themselves
    Inferior or superior [to others],
    And they should not take themselves as equal.   799

Letting go of what is grasped,[1]
    The person free of clinging
    Doesn't depend on knowledge

Or follow dissenting factions,
    Or fall back on any kind of view.   800

For those who are not inclined to either side
    Of becoming or non-becoming,
    Of here or the next world
    There exists nothing to get entrenched in
    When considering the doctrines others grasp.   801

Here, they have not even the slightest preconceived
        concepts[2]
    In regard to what is seen, heard, or thought out.
    How in this world could one categorize the Brahmin
    Who does not take hold of views?   802

They do not construct, prefer, or take up
    Any doctrines[3].
    A Brahmin not led by precepts or religious observances
    Who has gone beyond,
    Who is Thus,[4]
    Does not rely on belief.[5]   803

---

[1] In Pāli *atta* can mean either what is taken up or self. I have chosen the former because it fits the context better.

[2] "Concepts" here translates *saññā*—a word usually translated as "perception." Since the Buddhist meaning of *saññā* refers more to the label or conceptualization of what is perceived than it does to some pure act of perception, I have translated the term as "concept."

[3] "Doctrines" translates *dhamma*.

[4] *Tādī*

[5] "Rely on belief" translates *pacceti*. This word literally means "to come on to" or "to come back to." It has the extended meaning of to "rely on" or "to believe in." The commentary to the *Aṭṭhakavagga* gives "to experience again" and "to slide back to" as synonyms. It

Gil Fronsdal has practiced Zen and *Vipassanā* since 1975 and has a Ph.D. in Buddhist Studies from Stanford. He has trained in both the Japanese Soto Zen tradition and the Insight Meditation lineage of *Theravāda* Buddhism of Southeast Asia. He has been the primary teacher for the Insight Meditation Center in Redwood City, California since 1990 and is president of the Sati Center for Buddhist Studies. He is a husband and father of two boys.

---

explains that the Brahmin won't fall back into defilement (*Mahāniddesa* I.5).

Three Types of Wisdom: Study, Reflection, & Meditation

The Sati Journal Interviews Stephen Batchelor

SATI JOURNAL: The theme of the inaugural edition of the Sati Journal is the role of study in *Dhamma* practice. Do you have any general comments to make about this topic?

STEPHEN BATCHELOR: I think that there is a tendency within the Buddhist world, particularly in the West, to see study as an inessential adjunct to "practice." This reflects how much of the Western Buddhist community carries the legacy of the 1960s, which was an anti-intellectual, romantic movement that denigrated study and theory in favor of direct experience. It is understandable why that was the case at the time, but I think it is dangerous to perpetuate that view. It risks giving rise to a noncritical discussion of the Buddha's teaching in a way that doesn't give a reasoned, coherent account of what Buddhist practice is about. If there happen to be internal contradictions in what one says, that is not seen as being too big of a problem—after all, one might shrug, these are "just ideas."

Buddhist tradition, however, has a strong rational and critical thread running through it. The *Pāli* texts don't give the impression that the Buddha is a paradox-loving romantic. He is a very skilled dialectician. He argues and reasons with rigor and clarity, and has an enormous skill in using metaphor. He has a great sensitivity to the power of language and words and how to use them in transformative and often provocative ways. He was the source of the tradition that gave rise to great Buddhist thinkers, such as

Nāgārjuna, who developed the critical and rational side of the Buddha's teachings which gave rise to different schools of Buddhist philosophy.

Some of the most valuable parts of my own training as a monk were not in meditation skills but in dialectics, debate, and the rational analysis of texts. I found that extraordinarily helpful. As long as we are creatures who use language, we are bound to the principles of rationality and reason simply in order to make sense. If the Buddhist community is going to be able to communicate its ideas and values with the wider public, it needs to have a coherent and rational discourse. I think that if we abandon that, we do so at our own peril.

Study is integral to Buddhist practice. I remember a Mongolian lama called Geshe Ngawang Nyima with whom I studied once. He was teaching a class on Buddhist logic. Then someone asked him: "Geshe-la, why do we have to do all this study? Why can't we do more practice?" And he said: "If you really knew how to study, you would be practicing." To learn how to think clearly, to express oneself articulately: these are practices of the *Dhamma* in themselves.

Moreover, study enables us to enter into a closer relationship with the tradition. It provides us with a much clearer sense of where its ideas are coming from and how they are expressed. And modern scholarship, with its emphasis on historical criticism, helps us understand how the teachings attributed to the Buddha are often intelligible only as a critical response to the issues, ideas, and philosophical views of his time.

SATI: During the Buddha's time, study was conducted by oral transmission and today it is conducted through multiple media channels. Do you think that this has any bearing on the quality or scope of study?

BATCHELOR: No. These are just different ways of storing and retrieving information. Whether a text is written on paper, stored on the hard disc of a computer, or recorded in the neurological structure of your brain, it is always inscribed somewhere. Nonetheless, I am very glad that I memorized as much as I did. I have a considerable database of Buddhist doctrines and definitions of terms that were laid down in my twenties, and they are still accessible—though no doubt age and senility will wipe them out eventually. I find that memorized material is closer to hand. You are that much more intimate with it.

SATI: Do you encourage students to memorize texts?

BATCHELOR: No. It is not part of our culture and we are not trained to do it—besides which we have nearly instant access to a vast amount of material through the internet. Nonetheless, I think it is important for any serious practitioner to memorize the key Buddhist lists, such as the 4 truths, the 5 aggregates, the 12 links of dependent origination, the 4 foundations of mindfulness, and so on. This is useful both as a memory aid for reading the texts, and as providing themes for on-going reflection and contemplation. I am always rather shocked when I meet a Buddhist teacher who does not seem to have internalized at least these primary doctrines.

SATI: How has study informed your practice historically versus how you use study now to inform your meditation practice?

BATCHELOR: My involvement with Buddhism has always had a strong component of study. Much of my first years of training as a monk was taken up with in-depth study of classical Mahayana texts. One of the most intensive studies I did was of the

Bodhicariyāvatāra by Shantideva. I spent a year going methodically through that text and a 12th century Tibetan commentary to it with my teacher Geshe Dhargyey. Then I spent the next four years translating it into English. That was a very valuable experience. It enabled me to internalize somebody else's refined understanding of the *Dhamma* and to work very closely with it. Since I left the Tibetan tradition, I've not studied quite as systematically as that. In Korea, when I wasn't doing formal Zen practice, I spent a lot of time reading classical Zen records. In the last twenty years I have devoted myself to reading the *Suttas* and *Vinaya* of the *Pāli* Canon. I have also started learning *Pāli*—though I am very much an amateur and neophyte. I regret not having learned it when I was in my 20's; once you are past 50 it becomes that much more difficult to master another language.

Study informs my meditation practice by providing it with a clearer framework of meaning and purpose. In order to have meaning, experiences we have in meditation need be translated into some form of concepts and words. If we are practicing Buddhists, then surely we need to be as clear as we can about the Buddhist frameworks of meaning. In its broadest sense, practice involves two parallel processes: those of direct experience and conceptual and verbal articulation. These interfuse and interweave, sometimes in ways that are difficult to describe.

In *Dīgha Nikāya* 33 Sāriputta mentions three kinds of intelligence *(paññā)*. This is also a model I learned in the Tibetan tradition. There is intelligence that arises from hearing *(sutamayā paññā)*, intelligence that arises from thinking *(cintāmayā paññā)*, and intelligence that arises from cultivation or training *(bhāvanāmayā paññā)*. You start by hearing the teachings, thereby acquiring information. But information alone is inadequate. You then reflect upon what you have heard in a way that allows you to internalize it, so that it becomes part of a coherent and consistent view of oneself and the world. But this rational, conceptual exercise is still not enough. Whatever insights and understanding you have gained through such reflection need to be translated into actual felt experience. That is done through *bhāvanā*, cultivating yourself through meditative training so that what began as an idea is brought into being as a lived experience.

For example, you hear that all things are impermanent. That is just information. Then you think about the implications. "If I am impermanent, that means I am going to die." "Impermanence" then starts to become a key idea that informs how you make sense of who you are as person and what kind of world you live in. But it becomes an existential understanding only if you begin to directly experience the impermanence of things for yourself. You realize through mindful awareness that impermanence is a feature of your existence, rather than just an idea. By sensitizing yourself over time to this mark of being, it becomes integrated into your sense of who you are. I have always found this to be a useful way of presenting the process of *Vipassanā* meditation.

SATI: Do you have any recommendations for a beginner on where to start in using study to inform practice?

BATCHELOR: I would suggest that one start straightaway with the *suttas* themselves, rather than later commentarial works. My first exposure to the *Pāli suttas* was Ñāṇamoli Thera's *The Life of the Buddha*. I read this while I was a Tibetan Buddhist monk, and it opened up the world of the *Pāli* canon for me. It is a marvelous anthology of key canonical texts. Bhikkhu Bodhi's *In the Buddha's Words* is also an anthology well worth studying. The problem with any anthology, however, is that it will unavoidably reflect the preferences of the author or the orthodoxy to which he or she belongs, which may not correspond with your own interests and needs. Yet simply to plunge straight into the canon can be rather daunting and bewildering simply because there is so much material. In my own case, I found the *suttas* that concerned Mara to be particularly helpful, but neither of the anthologies I've mentioned gives them much importance. At some point, you are probably just going to have to follow your own nose. You need to find those texts that speak to your own condition, rather than feel religiously bound to read those *suttas* that tradition has deemed important.

At the beginning it is useful to find a teacher who can help you find your way through this morass of texts. Once you get a toehold into the body of material, you can more easily pursue your study yourself, by looking up related passages where the Buddha or one of his monks expands and elaborates on the theme that engages you. This will require a certain amount of leg work, some of which might lead you up blind alleys, but if you persist, you will find that after a while your study becomes a kind of adventure, which can lead you to remarkable discoveries and insights. If study is to become a practice, then it needs to become an open-ended quest of following your own intuitions. I think that is how it should be. But orthodoxies tend to say, "This is what the Buddha's teachings really mean," then selectively give readings that support the orthodox view. That can be a useful starting point, but if we are really going to get into this material, we have to make it our own.

SATI: You mentioned earlier that you have studied *Pāli*. Do you think that is important to study the texts in their original languages?

BATCHELOR: I'm afraid it is. English translations, no matter how competent the translator, will always leave you one step removed from the original. You will inevitably be subject to the biases of the translator. All translation, as the cliché goes, is interpretation

We are very fortunate in that we have so many different translations of the primary *Pāli* texts available in English. If you are studying a *sutta*, read as many different versions as you can. Don't just rely on one translator. That will allow you to see the different shades of meaning a single word in *Pāli* can possess. Each translator helps you get a sense of the nuances of a given *Pāli* word. Any term in a classical language is unlikely to have an exact, one-to-one equivalent with an English term. Yet the translator is always obliged to select one English word among several possible options. In addition, the chosen English word is very likely to carry associations that the *Pāli* word doesn't. It will have resonances for you as an English speaker that the *Pāli* word may not have for a *Pāli* reader.

SATI: Do you see a movement among contemporary Western *Vipassanā* teachers or other contemporary Buddhist teachers toward advocating study to their students?

BATCHELOR: Well, some do, and some don't. But I wouldn't say I see a movement. In the dedicated practitioner programs offered at Spirit Rock, for example, there is recognition that to understand the *Dhamma* you need to do more than just become proficient in mindfulness, so a certain emphasis is given to gaining some knowledge of the traditional texts. But I still have the impression that study and thinking are seen as something optional, an adjunct to what really counts, i.e. meditation. On the other hand, I don't see why meditators should be forced to study *Pāli* texts if that doesn't suit their temperament or fit with their way of incorporating their practices into their lives.

There is still this common idea that texts only provide concepts, but what really matters is your own experience. This may be true to a point. But "experience" is a vague and tricky term. Your experience might be nothing more than your own highly subjective and idiosyncratic take on something. My experience of meditation has always served as a conversation partner with my knowledge of the textual tradition. I see the two as having an interactive relationship. I would certainly not just trust my experience alone. I would always want to check it against the wisdom of the tradition. On the other hand I wouldn't want to be slavishly devoted to the authority of a textual tradition without it having any connection to my own life. In other words, *Dhamma* practice is an on-going conversation, even an argument with tradition. You meditate, you do retreats, then you go back to the texts and reflect further on their meaning. That helps inform, clarify, and integrate your experiences so that when you return to the cushion, you bring that knowledge of the tradition with you in a subliminal way.

SATI: Do you encourage the study of the traditional commentaries? What about more contemporary writings on Buddhism?

BATCHELOR: I don't believe that any one commentarial tradition has the final word on the meaning of the primary canonical texts. I am not a Theravādin, and I do not hold Buddhaghosa's fifth century commentaries in any particular esteem. There is also much to be learned from scholars such as Richard Gombrich, who are not necessarily practicing Buddhists, but have made a lifelong study of the canonical texts using Western historical-critical methods. Gombrich and others seek to locate the Buddha's *suttas* in the context of 5th century B.C.E. India, where they were taught. I feel this is crucial for our understanding of the *Dhamma*. The Buddha did not teach in a vacuum or from some transcendental perspective, but in the context of a culture, in response to particular beliefs held at the time, in dialogue with people from a specific kind of society. Modern scholarship is now able to tell us a great deal about the kind of world in which the Buddha worked.

SATI: What are some pitfalls of combining study with meditation practice?

BATCHELOR: Well, I suppose you could get carried away, and put off your meditation because you are more fascinated with some technical problem in *Pāli* grammar. But if your approach to the *Dhamma* involves a personal commitment, and you keep your broader goals in perspective, you will be fine. If you have a good teacher and a supportive community, that should be sufficient to prevent you from becoming either a blinkered meditator or a neurotic scholar.

SATI: Can study lead to discursive thinking and *papañca*?

BATCHELOR: You mean meditation can't? Scholar and meditator alike have to be alert to their own tendencies to an unnecessary proliferation of thoughts. I don't think that study is more or less prone to these things than meditation. You can sit in meditation while your mind wanders all over the place, generating all sorts of fantastical theories and stories. This kind of objection to study again reflects the anti-intellectual, romantic bias of many students of Buddhism. We really have to get over that and try to reach a more integrated notion of study-practice rather than constantly being suspicious that study is going to take us away from the path. Why don't we worry that meditation might take us away from the path? There are just as many pitfalls in practicing meditation; we can end up in all kinds of weird and self-deluding states. Study and careful reflection, however, can serve as a useful safeguard against such perils.

SATI: In your most recent book *Confession of a Buddhist Atheist* you give a secular interpretation of the life of the Buddha as represented in the *Pāli suttas* that differs from the traditional, more religious or mythological approach that has been taught historically. How do you think that your pragmatic approach will affect how Western students study and practice the *Dhamma*?

BATCHELOR: Well, it may have no effect at all. That depends on whether students are willing to take my writing seriously. For myself, I have found that the more human the Buddha becomes, the more his teachings connect to experience in the real world and are less of a prescription for transcendence. The Buddha's life is in itself a teaching of the *Dhamma*. It shows us how the Buddha addressed the specific situations of his socio-political world. It demonstrates how he was not indifferent to the plight of that world. He was constantly involved with people: not just his monks but powerful rulers, wealthy merchants, religious opponents, simple farmers, his ambitious relatives. He had to do whatever was necessary to ensure the survival of his teachings and community. The *suttas* show us how the Buddha taught not just by words but by his actions. The Buddha struggled with the same sort of issues and conflicts much as we do. He was beset by all manner of crises, threats, scandals, and compromises.

By humanizing the Buddha, one humanizes the *Dhamma*. This does not mean, however, that one should reject the well-known mythic accounts of his life. The story of Prince Siddhattha growing up in his palace and seeing the four sights is a powerful universal myth that speaks to the core existential dilemma of humankind. But it says nothing about Siddhattha Gotama's life as the eldest son of a local oligarch in a failing republic in 5th century B.C.E. Kosala. As long as we don't confuse myth with history, we can appreciate the value of both.

As a westerner, I am formed both by a secular tradition that values historicity and a religious tradition where the narrative of Jesus' life plays a central role in his message. You cannot separate the teachings of Jesus in the gospels from the drama of his life. The life is the teaching. The same is true of much the Old Testament as well. But that narrative dimension has never been given much attention in Buddhism. You have the legend of how Siddhattha Gotama became the Buddha. Then you have the *Dhamma*. After the awakening, you hear about a number of disconnected episodes, whose main purpose is to set the scene for a teaching, and finally the Buddha dies in Kusinara. I wonder if this is one of the reasons why Buddhism has often tended toward abstraction, transcendence, and an indifference to the affairs of the world.

So in one way, what I am doing in this book is giving a historically conscious reading of the Buddha's life. I am searching for a gospel-like narrative that can weave the threads of teaching together with those of the life. My quest for the historical Buddha has served to ground his teaching in the world. The model of the Buddha's life also challenges me to apply the *Dhamma* in the social, economic, political, and religious context in which we live. It is an unapologetically pragmatic and secular approach. If Buddhists choose to model their lives on the liberated *arahant*—or the idealized Mahayana *bodhisattva*, for that matter—rather than follow the example of Siddhattha Gotama, then I wonder how Buddhism will find a compelling voice to address the pressing issues of our world today. That is important. I don't want Buddhism to become ghettoized.

SATI: What do you mean by "ghettoized?"

BATCHELOR: I mean you get lots of Buddhist groups that are absorbed in what they are doing but have relatively little interaction with the wider world of which they are a part. To some extent this is inevitable with any new religious movement. We are still working towards a Western Buddhist language and identity, to a time when Buddhists will no longer be perceived as some sort of alien presence. We have some way to go before the average person walking down the street doesn't do a second take when a non-Asian like me announces that he is a Buddhist.

SATI: In our culture, in addition to Christianity we have the religion of psychology. What do you think of the impact of Western psychology on Buddhism in America?

BATCHELOR: If you look at how Buddhism has entered into different cultures in the past, it has tended to find points of common interest within the new host culture. In the case of China, for example, Buddhism attracted Taoists, who had an interest in meditation. In the secular West, it is hardly surprising that Buddhism attracts those interested in psychology. The Buddhist analysis of the causes of suffering, for example, immediately strikes us as psychologically astute. But it is a two-way process. As Buddhist teachers recognize the interest among psychologists and therapists, they tend to highlight the psychological aspects of the *Dhamma*, more so than would be the case when teaching in traditional Asian societies. On the other hand, it would be alarming if Buddhism in the West were to be over-determined by psychological discourse, and Buddhism evolved into a kind of spiritual psychotherapy. That would be far too reductive. The practice of the *Dhamma* embraces the totality of the eightfold path. It is an integral way of life that balances philosophical insight, ethical commitment, right livelihood, spiritual discipline, and the forming of community. To over-emphasize its psychological dimension risks losing sight of its complex reality as a culture that addresses every aspect of human need.

SATI: How can we know which parts of the Brahmanical tradition the Buddha accepted and which he rejected?

BATCHELOR: It is very important that we understand the Buddha's teachings in the context of his times. And there is plenty of material in the canon where the Buddha seems to accept elements of traditional Indian belief. Yet I must confess that what I find least appealing and helpful in Buddhism are precisely those elements it shares with Hinduism: rebirth, karma as a scheme of moral book-keeping, the goal of freeing oneself from the cycle of birth and death, the idea that there is a transcendent consciousness or absolute that underpins phenomenal experience. Not only do these ideas not speak to me, they often seem to obscure what was truly original and distinctive in what the Buddha taught: the principle of conditioned arising, the four noble truths, mindful awareness of phenomenal experience, and the emphasis on self-reliance. I admit that my approach is subjective. I am concerned with those teachings and texts that address my condition as a human being here and now, and provide an inspiring and practical framework for living in this world.

I don't believe the Buddha had a detailed metaphysical theory that he sought to impose on the world irrespective of whom he was addressing. He was a situationalist. His teachings were given to specific people in specific situations at specific times in their lives. He considered himself a physician, and his *Dhamma* a medicine. He prescribed different treatments to different people in different situations. That is the great message of the Buddha's teaching. It is not dogmatic or doctrinaire but therapeutic and pragmatic. Of course, I am following my own intuitions as to what is universal in his vision of what human life could be. I am not interested in those teachings that are intelligible only to those who uphold an Indian world view. I doubt Buddhism will get very far in the modern world if one insists that to really understand and practice it you have first to embrace the cosmology of ancient India. Such an insistence is likely to condemn Buddhism to marginality. Nor do I believe that science will one day finally vindicate these dogmas. That is clutching at straws. Perhaps the Buddha did believe in some of these things. I don't find that problematic - like all people he was a product of his time, and the teachings he gave were embedded to some degree in the context of his Indian culture. But I don't think those beliefs are what is really universal and liberating about the Buddha's *Dhamma*.

Stephen Batchelor is a former monk in the Tibetan and Korean Zen traditions. He teaches meditation and Buddhism worldwide and is the author of many books, including *Buddhism without Beliefs, Living with the Devil,* and *Confession of a Buddhist Atheist.* For more information visit his website at: www.stephenbatchelor.org.

Informing Practice Through Study

RICHARD SHANKMAN

UPON EMBARKING ON ANY COURSE we need to understand what we are undertaking and why. This is especially true for endeavors of great consequence, such as Dharma practice, which have the power to reshape our lives in radical ways. Buddhist contemplative practices challenge our fundamental assumptions about ourselves, our experience, and our relationship with the world around us.

If we begin meditation, or Dharma practice in any of its forms, without some perspective and framework from which to apply ourselves, our experience will unfold by chance and take us in its own direction according to our predilections and tendencies. We need to understand the purposes of Buddhist teachings and practices in order to make wise and informed choices and assess what is skillful action. Dharma unfolds uniquely for each of us. A contextual basis within which to understand what is happening and where we are going acts as a protector and guide. Without knowing where we are heading, we can often create unnecessary suffering along this path intended to lead to an end of suffering. An appreciation of the potentials, limitations, and pitfalls of whatever teachings and practices we engage in acts as an ally to inform our choices and guide how we direct our efforts.

I have had the opportunity to study and practice with a number of teachers in various Buddhist and non-Buddhist contemplative traditions, all of whom were quite different in style and content, in the practices they were teaching, and in their understanding of the goals and reasons for undertaking spiritual practices. Some were openly critical of other teachers and traditions, believing that they held the correct understanding of the true path of the spiritual life. Others were genuinely accepting and appreciative of other approaches, realizing that there are many ways to come to liberation and that there is not a single right or best path of practice, only whichever approach works best for each of us according to our individual nature and disposition.

When I began meditation practice in 1970 I was young and idealistic, without much basis for understanding the teachings. I had a vague idea of what I was seeking but little idea of the foundational teachings or goals of the practices I was undertaking. As I studied with various teachers and engaged in a variety of practices, I began to piece together a conceptual basis within which to understand what I was doing and why. Only later did I delve systematically into a thorough study of Buddhist teachings, history, and development.

The more teachings and trainings I was exposed to, especially when informed by inquiry and study, the more I understood the overall context for what I was doing. It seemed the less I knew and grasped about the range and diversity of teachings, practice styles, and goals, the more rigidly I held to certain attitudes and the more sure I was of my beliefs and views. I used to have very strong judgments and opinions about the right way to practice, the right understanding and interpretations of the path, and where the practice was heading. The more I've learned and been exposed to, the more open, receptive, and truly appreciative I've become of the great mosaic of effective methods and skillful means.

As I became more educated and my understanding matured, my appreciation for the range of skillful means broadened. I saw that some practices, which worked very well for certain people, were just not a good fit for others. People seemed to have attained deep states of realization and awakening practicing in all the various styles and practices I encountered. I realized that it is not a matter of finding the right, true practice, as if there were such a thing waiting for us to discover, but finding the practice that is best for each of us. This served only to inform and strengthen my own practice.

The early *Sangha* did not practice in a vacuum, without an understanding of what they were doing or why. The Buddha, as recorded in the *Pāli* literature, did not only give meditation instructions. The entire *Pāli* canon is a compilation of teachings on the principles and application of Dharma practice from the Buddha and other senior disciples. Throughout his teaching career, from the time of his enlightenment until his death, the Buddha engaged in various skillful means for conveying the path and practice of liberation, presenting a framework within which to understand what they were undertaking and to set clear intentions and a context within which to hold the practice.

In those days, study looked quite different from what we may be used to today, consisting not in immersion in books, but of direct individual guidance and instruction; teachings were preserved and transmitted in an oral form, through personal transmission and presence. In the stories preserved and handed down to us from those times, senior disciples would spend hours teaching and would sometimes stay up all night discussing Dharma. From those early times and continuing throughout the history of Buddhism, practice has always been understood to be properly accompanied and informed by study to some degree.

Practices that calm the mind, open the heart, and strengthen mindfulness and clear awareness can be applied toward any goal. What makes practice Buddhist, rather than secular, is the end toward which these qualities are directed. The application of

Dharma practices generally improves our lives. The cultivation of mindfulness is extremely effective for reducing stress, increasing well-being, and improving concentration in any endeavor. If we can train our minds to be more relaxed, spacious, and loving, we will feel happier and our interactions with others will be easier and more pleasant. If we do not understand the aim of Buddhist teachings, which point to a complete release and end to suffering, then in our efforts to decrease stress, live with more ease, and rid ourselves of unpleasant experiences, we may miss the greater possibility of liberation from suffering that is independent of conditions. In an attempt to shift the conditions of our lives we may never learn to turn towards and meet our suffering, to come to know and understand it, and to be present and free in the midst of the reality of each moment.

Educating ourselves about the goals of practice can help unmask unexamined assumptions about ourselves and the teachings, which in turn sheds light on our motivations for practicing. Levels of clinging and identity we may have not been aware of can be revealed which, in turn, can inform clarity of intention.

As our Dharma practice develops we can become confused when we hear conflicting teachings or we enter new and unfamiliar territory in our meditation. It helps to have a map of the terrain, both in terms of meditative experiences and in applying Dharma teachings to the range of daily life situations. There is a rich array of teachings and reflections from others who have gone before us, and we can often avoid needless suffering and wasted time by familiarizing ourselves with their roadmaps for how the practical applications of the teachings can evolve. I was motivated to write my book *The Experience of Samādhi* precisely because there was so much confusion and misinformation floating around about the topic of samādhi (concentration) and its relation to meditation practice.

We may engage in various styles of learning, depending on our interests and needs, ranging from listening to a Dharma talk or receiving basic meditation instructions to formal, structured study, individually or in small or large group settings. Irrespective of the form of study we engage in, most importantly, the process should be relevant and applicable to our meditative and everyday experience. All of the Buddha's teachings and practices – the entire Dharma - are not meant for intellectual understanding alone, but are intended to be applied directly in our daily lives. Study of Buddhist doctrine, history, and development may be interesting for its own sake, but if undertaken merely as an academic exercise, disconnected from and not applied to our lived experience, we miss the real worth and personal benefit it can bring. Study is of tremendous value and great reward if it informs how we think and act and brings us to a direct experiential knowing, applied directly to meet our daily lives.

Ajahn Chah, the greatly respected and beloved Thai meditation master, compared study without practical application to a ladle in a pot of soup. The ladle is in the soup, but it does not know the taste of soup. We can absorb ourselves in study, but if we want to taste the Dharma, if we wish to experience and embody the love, compassion, wisdom, and liberation pointed to by the Buddha, the teachings must be put into practice.

Richard Shankman has been a meditator since 1970 and teaches at Dharma centers and groups throughout the San Francisco Bay Area and nationally. He is a co-founder of the Sati Center for Buddhist Studies and of Mindful Schools. Richard is the author of "The Experience of Samādhi: An In-Depth Investigation of Buddhist Meditation." For more information please visit his website at www.richardshankman.org.

Book Review: What the Buddha Thought

RICHARD GOMBRICH

Oxford Centre for Buddhist Studies Monographs
Equinox 2009; 240 pp., $24.95 (paper)

REVIEWED BY TONY BERNHARD

IN THE ĀṆI SUTTA: THE PEG (SN 20.7) the Buddha warns of a future in which his teachings are clouded by the confusion of re-interpretation and commentary:

> [people] will listen when discourses that are literary works—the works of poets, elegant in sound, elegant in rhetoric, the work of outsiders, words of disciples—are recited. They will lend ear and set their hearts on knowing them. They will regard these teachings as worth grasping and mastering. In this way the disappearance of the discourses that are words of the Tathagata—deep, deep in their meaning, transcendent, connected with emptiness—will come about.

Richard Gombrich, the Boden Professor of Sanskrit at Oxford University (1976-2004) and the president of the *Pāli* Text Society from 1995-2002, brings the disciplined skills of contemporary scholarship to the study of primary-source *Pāli* texts while placing them in their original historical setting. The results contain significant surprises that are substantial enough for the last chapter of the book to be titled "Is This Book to be Believed?"

The title of the book itself, *What the Buddha Thought*, is an intentional word play on the classic work by Rahula Walpola, *What the Buddha Taught,* and thus exemplifies the word play, irony and metaphor that Gombrich asserts were essential hallmarks of the Buddha's teaching style. Today's 'official' version of the Buddha's teachings might, Gombrich quips, be more aptly characterized as "What Buddhaghosa Taught" after the 5th century Sri Lankan monk who assembled the authoritative commentaries for the Theravādin tradition.

Gombrich aims to restore the meanings lost by later commentators—Buddhaghosa most particularly—who lost touch with the world in which the Buddha himself lived and thus sought meaning in the words of the texts themselves rather than looking to situationally based meanings. "Many of [the Buddha's] ideas were formulated," he says, "to refute other ideas current in his day, but to put them across, he had inevitably to use the language of his opponents, for he had no other."

One example that Gombrich uses to illustrate this process is the Buddha's use of the word *upādāna* which is usually rendered as "grasping" or "clinging." As used by the Brahmans of the time, *upādāna* referred to the ritual stoking of three sacred fires that were kept burning in Brahmanical households. The Buddha hijacked the word and changed its meaning to describe the act of feeding the fires of greed, hatred, and delusion rather than three sacred fires. By transferring the reference of the term from a ritually enacted performance, the Buddha used *upādāna* to illustrate the way our actions lead to suffering.

For the Buddha of the *Pāli* Canon, ritual activity itself was useless, though that notion has been somewhat modified by later commentators who attribute "skillful means" to some kinds of habitual, ritualized activity. In any case, for the Brahmans of the Buddha's time, ritual was all important for it was through correctly performed ritual that harmonious living in the universe was maintained. Because exact performance was important, there was particular emphasis on the precision with which each ritual was executed. The correct performance of a ritual act was denoted by the word *karman*.

The Buddha took the Bramanical word for ritual and used it to denote ethical intention: *karma* is intention, he declared. Ethicizing behavior in this way was a huge paradigm shift from the prevailing sensibilities of his time and it was one of the major doctrinal element that set him apart from his Brahman and Jain contemporaries.

The most basic elements of Vedic teachings—that ultimately we are nothing but being, consciousness, and bliss— appear almost unintelligible to the Buddha that Gombrich describes. The Buddha was uninterested in what we would term metaphysics—philosophizing about what really exists—but was instead engaged in what we would term phenomenology—the examination of what is present for consciousness.

Consciousness or awareness isn't a thing in the Buddha's Dharma: it is simply a conditioned process. Such entities as "pure consciousness" or "universal spirit"—unconditioned, self-contained, and ultimately satisfying to experience—don't appear in the *Pāli* Canon. The Buddha was not concerned with 'things' because processes are all we experience and so, to point to experience which eludes conventional, denotative language, he relied on metaphor and analogy.

However, when you take metaphor and analogy—not to mention irony—out of context and attempt to analyze the words in which the teachings are presented, it's easy to miss the metaphoric qualities and to become more literal minded.

The word Nibbana itself, for example, the goal of practice, is also a process, Gombrich says. It is something we do: the word is an intransitive verb that translates as "going out" or "extinguishing," referring to process of allowing the fires of greed, hatred, delusion to die out. It can be confusing to treat it as a noun, a thing, an entity in itself because as a thing, it becomes something to be acquired and an unconditioned entity, it can easily appear to be well out of reach of our constantly changing experience.

Perhaps the most striking example of Gombrich's exploration of metaphor in the Buddha's teachings comes in his discussion of the *Brahma Vihāras*—especially mettā—which we understand as a simple, though desirable, mental state. Gombrich says, however, that for any Brahman at the time, the notion of dwelling with Brahma would have been readily understood as the achievement of the ultimate goal. The *Brahma Vihāras*, says Gombrich, would be the qualities of a fully awakened one, and the cultivation of the *Brahma Vihāras* are a fully effective path to full awakening.

This may not be a common understanding today. The *Brahma Vihāras* are taught as a skillful method of cultivating concentration and desireable mental states. This, according to Gombrich, is the result of the commentators having lost contact with the life and times of the Buddha. The *mettā sutta*, he points out, describes one who knows the path of peace, one who has awakened and will not be born again into the world: a description of an arahant or non-returner.

Seeking the meaning of the passage in the words themselves rather than in looking to what they would have meant in the Buddha's time is the result of abstracted and literal thinking about the texts unconnected with the context in which they were uttered. Grasping the teachings as you would a snake, Gombrich says, if done incorrectly (i.e. taking the texts literally when they were meant metaphorically) can result in getting bitten by delusion.

Is this book to be believed? As you might imagine, this is more a work of academic prose than of poetry. It is the result of disciplined scholarship that is well worth the effort to study. For those of us who do not have the academic credentials to evaluate his work critically, Gombrich's presentation shines a new light on the Buddha's teachings, and in that light there is a lot to explore.

Tony Bernhard is one of Spirit Rock's Community Dharma Leaders. He sits on the board of the Sati Center for Buddhist Studies, is a member of the Spirit Rock Meditation Center Planning Committee and hosts sitting groups and teaches Dharma in Davis, CA.

Online Resources for Dhamma Study

Sutta Translations:

Access to Insight - a databank of *sutta* translations, study guides, and *Dhamma* essays:

> www.accesstoinsight.org

Sutta Discovery - Piya Tan's annotated *sutta* translations and study guides:

> dharmafarer.org

Sutta Central - An online *sutta* database in English, *Pāli*, Chinese, Tibetan, and other modern languages:

> www.suttacentral.net/

Wikipitaka – Online open-source English translation of the *Pāli Tipiṭaka.*

> tipitaka.wikia.com/wiki/Main_Page

Ancient Buddhist Texts - *Sutta* translations, maps, and study guides by Bhikkhu Ānandajoti:

> www.ancient-buddhist-texts.net/index.htm

The *Pāli* Canon - The *Vipassanā* Fellowship online *Pāli* Canon database:

www.vipassana.com/canon/

Internet Sacred Texts Archive - English translation of parts of the *Pāli* Canon by T.W. Rhys Davids and others:

sacred-texts.com/bud/index.htm

Pāli Canon Databanks:

Online Searchable *Pāli* Canon databases which are based on the *Chaṭṭha Saṅgāyana*:

www.tipitaka.org/

studies.worldtipitaka.org/

Online *Pāli* canon and English translation by Sister Upalavanna at Mettānet:

www.metta.lk/tipitaka/index.html

Dictionaries:

The *Pāli* Text Society's online *Pāli* -English Dictionary:

dsal.uchicago.edu/dictionaries/pali/

Manual of Buddhist Terms and Doctrines by Nyanatiloka:

www.palikanon.com/english/wtb/dic_idx.html

Buddhist Dictionary of *Pāli* Proper Names:

www.palikanon.com/english/*Pāli*_names/dic_idx.html

Critical *Pāli* Dictionary:

pali.hum.ku.dk/cpd/

Sutta Study Guides:

U Ko Lay's *"Guide to the Tipitaka"*:

www.buddhanet.net/pdf_file/tipitaka.pdf

Sharda Rogell's "Pressing Out Pure Honey" guide to the *Majjhima Nikāya*:

www.dharma.org/bcbs/Pages/documents/PressingOutPure

Honey.pdf

Sati Center *sutta* study course audio recordings and study guides by Gil Fronsdal and others:

www.sati.org

Andrew Olendzki's *Mettā Sutta* study guide:

www.dharma.org/bcbs/ReadingRoom.html

Audio:

Sutta Readings - selected suttas read aloud by various *Dhamma* teachers:

www.suttareadings.net/index.html

An audio *Pāli* word pronunciation dictionary:

studies.worldtipitaka.org/audio_alpha

Bhikkhu Bodhi's recordings on *sutta* studies and *Pāli* lessons:

www.bodhimonastery.net/bm/about-

buddhism/audio.html

Offline Searchable Databanks:

Searchable *Pāli* glossary and *sutta* database by Leigh Brasington

www.leighb.com/glossary.htm

www.leighb.com/suttadb.htm

Digital *Pāli* Reader by Bhikkhu Yuttadhammo with *Pāli* Canon and Commentaries database and dictionaries for translating *Pāli* texts:

pali.sirimangalo.org

Books:

Pariyatti - seller of Buddhist books including publications from the *Pāli* Text Society and the Buddhist Publication Society:

www.pariyatti.org

Buddhist Publication Society – online versions of essays and books relevant to *sutta* study:

www.bps.lk/index.asp

Wisdom Publications:

www.wisdompubs.org

Pāli studies:

> www.tipitaka.net/pali/

> *Pāli*.pratyeka.org/

> www.nibbanam.com/pali_language_tools.html

Miscellaneous:

Buddhanet – Online Buddhist texts and information:

> www.buddhanet.net/

Digital Sanskrit Buddhist Canon:

> www.uwest.edu/sanskritcanon/dp/

Essays and translations by Ven. Thanissaro Bhikkhu:

> www.dhammatalks.org/

Dharmanet:

> www.dharmanet.org/

The Sati Center for Buddhist Studies

The Sati Center supports the study of Buddhist teachings. Our perspective balances scholarly inquiry with serious meditation practice. We believe that study and practice work together to deepen one's practice and aid in awakening. Our goal is to help participants explore original Buddhist texts and appreciate the richness of the tradition and lineage. We want to facilitate ongoing dialog and exchange among meditators, teachers, students and scholars. We offer daylong classes, *Dhamma* study publications, and online study materials.

Faculty of the Sati Center (Current and Former):

Gil Fronsdal
Andrea Fella
Ven. Thanissaro Bhikkhu
Ven. Bhikkhu Bodhi
John Peacock
Stephen Batchelor
Richard Shankman
Leigh Brasington
Nona Olivia
Jennifer Block
Jaku Kinst
Ven. Anālayo

Donald Rothberg
Martine Batchelor
Paul Haller
Jacque Verduin
Ajahn Amaro
Rick Hanson
Bhante Gunaratana
Joan DePaoli
Steve Armstrong
Santikaro
Norman Fisher

Support the Publication of the Sati Journal

Since the days of the Buddha, the teachings have been considered priceless, and thus offered freely whenever possible. Daylong classes and the Sutta Study Program are offered by donation and everyone is welcome.

DONATIONS are used to make offerings to the teachers and to pay the expenses of putting on the classes.

If you wish to support the publication of the *Sati Journal* or other programs at the Sati Center please visit our website to make a donation through PayPal on our website (www.sati.org) or you can mail a check to us at:

The Sati Center for Buddhist Studies
108 Birch Street
Redwood City, CA 94062
Email: satijournal@sati.org

We also are in need of VOLUNTEERS to help edit, publish, and distribute the Sati Journal. Please contact us if you would like to help.

Sati Institute for Theravāda Buddhist Studies (SITBS)

The Sati Center for Buddhist Studies announces the creation of SITBS, the first Western degree-granting institution of *Theravāda* Buddhist learning. In collaboration with the Institute of Buddhist Studies, we will be offering courses toward a Masters of Buddhist Studies (M.B.S.) degree. The program is designed for those interested in a systematic education in *Theravāda* Buddhist Studies for professional or personal purposes.

Buddhist Chaplaincy Training Program at the Sati Center

As Buddhist spiritual practice finds an increasing presence within American society, there is both an opportunity and a need to train Buddhist practitioners to serve as spiritual caregivers and chaplains. The Sati Center for Buddhist Studies is offering a yearlong training program to provide an introduction to spiritual care skills from a Buddhist perspective. This is a unique opportunity to study Buddhist principles and practices relevant to spiritual caregiving, as well as an introduction to the psychological, social, and ethical issues related to chaplaincy.